DIGGING
DEEPER

Other Books by Laurie Hyatt, PhD

Silent Decision: Awareness Out of Tragedy
Think Your Way to Happiness: Strategies for an Enjoyable, Meaningful Life
Tools for Living: Taking Control of your Life, Second Edition

Digging Deeper

Finding Myself on Hopi and Navajo Land

Laurie Hyatt, PhD

BOOKLOGIX®
Alpharetta, Georgia

The author has tried to recreate events, locations, and conversations from his/her memories of them. In some instances, in order to maintain their anonymity, the author has changed the names of individuals and places. He/she may also have changed some identifying characteristics and details such as physical attributes, occupations, and places of residence.

Copyright © 2024 by Laurie Hyatt

All rights reserved. No part of this book may be reproduced or transmitted in any form or by any means, electronic or mechanical, including photocopying, recording, or any information storage and retrieval system, without permission in writing from the author.

ISBN: 978-1-6653-0763-5 - Paperback
eISBN: 978-1-6653-0764-2 - eBook

These ISBNs are the property of BookLogix for the express purpose of sales and distribution of this title. The content of this book is the property of the copyright holder only. BookLogix does not hold any ownership of the content of this book and is not liable in any way for the materials contained within. The views and opinions expressed in this book are the property of the Author/Copyright holder, and do not necessarily reflect those of BookLogix.

☉This paper meets the requirements of ANSI/NISO Z39.48-1992 (Permanence of Paper)

1 2 2 8 2 3

This book is dedicated to . . .

My mother, Marjorie Virginia Chapman Innes (1914–1983). She was an artist, musician, book lover, ice skater, swimmer, sailor, gardener, patio builder, daughter, sister, wife, and mother.

Here's to your rebellious spirit, your selfless devotion as a mother, your unfulfilled dreams, and to the dreams that came to fruition because you took the risk to leave the comfortable and familiar behind and travel toward the unknown, welcoming challenges and searching for a life yet unimagined.

Contents

Author's Note		ix
Prologue		1
Chapter 1	Feeling Free	7
Chapter 2	Building A Community	11
Chapter 3	Solitude	15
Chapter 4	Kindred Spirits	19
Chapter 5	Off the Beaten Path	29
Chapter 6	Why Start a Women's Circle?	47
Chapter 7	What Brought Me to This Place?	59
Chapter 8	Flying Free	65
Chapter 9	Letters from Daddy	75
Chapter 10	Onward and Upward	95
Chapter 11	Arizona	101
Chapter 12	From Flagstaff to the Hopi Land	115
Chapter 13	Sacred Hopi Land, Special Hopi People	125
Chapter 14	Hopi Beliefs, Hopi Resourcefulness, Hopi Creativity	137
Chapter 15	An Author Is Born	147
Chapter 16	Humbled by the Kiva Ceremony	155
Chapter 17	A Mystical Experience in the Dark of Night	163

Chapter 18	**The San Francisco Peaks and the Full Moon**	171
Chapter 19	**Out of Balance**	177
Chapter 20	**Window Rock**	181

Epilogue 187

Author's Note

Before I began writing this book, I gathered my photos, personal journals, letters, and newspaper articles to help me remember people, places, and events and to add to the accuracy of my words. During the time that I was writing, I also talked with many people who were included in the book, some by phone and some by driving to meet with them. I drove to Ellijay to look again at some of the places that I described.

I relied mostly on my memory of events and my memory of the chronology of events. I researched some data, including some mileage distances and some names of places that I could not recall.

I did not change the names of any individuals and there are no composite characters or events in the book. Many people that I knew or events that happened during the time period 1994 to 1999 were not included because they did not relate to the theme of the story.

This book focuses on a time in my life when I engaged in an intense search for the meaning of my life. It's just a glimpse of the full story.

PROLOGUE

I was a forty-seven-year-old recently divorced woman in 1994 when I sat on my black-and-silver 250 cc motorcycle at the top of my steep, curved, dirt driveway, fingers clutching the brake. Dressed in a black leather jacket, black jeans, and boots, my sunglasses disguised my blue eyes and my black helmet hid most of my wavy blonde hair. Today I planned to experience the freedom and thrill and "coolness" of riding to town sans doors and windows. It was a pretty fall day in the North Georgia Mountains, a good day for a ride.

As I stared down the forty-five-degree descent, I got more and more scared. What had seemed possible when I mounted the motorcycle moments before now seemed terrifying. Not only the steep descent, but halfway down there was a forty-five-degree turn to the left, with no shoulder if I miscalculated.

I shifted positions, thinking that would give my mind the green light. Still sitting. I asked myself why I bought this motorcycle if I wasn't going to ride it. But that didn't work either. All the shifting and self-talk didn't override my panic. I just sat there, looking at the steep dirt driveway and the curve about halfway down. I sat there for a long time and, finally, I gave up. With a big sigh and lots of frustration with myself, I got off my motorcycle and, holding the handlebars, pushed it back into the basement. I would eventually muster the courage, but not that day.

When I moved to Ellijay, known for its numerous apple farms and breathtaking mountain views, I knew no one except Tom, the contractor who initially told me about a beautiful piece of property that a builder, Sam, was going to use for a spec house. "I think he would sell it to you if he can build the house," he said over the phone. "The lot is in a nice community called Walnut Mountain that has wonderful spring water and a big community swimming pool."

We rode up to look at the mountainside lot and meet Sam on a Saturday in April. White mountain laurel and pink azaleas were everywhere and the sound of the water babbling over rocks in the creek that formed one of the property lines was music to my ears. I was hooked. After Sam and I were introduced, he made me an intriguing offer. "I'll sell you this lot and build a six-hundred-square-foot real log cabin with a basement for fifty-five thousand." Tom added, "Laurie, I know that we had talked about a three-hundred-twenty-square-foot plan, but in Walnut Mountain, the minimum square footage allowed is six hundred square feet. And now you can have a second bedroom and a bigger living room." I thought about it for a few minutes. We had a deal.

Before I could catch my breath, Sam and his crew were hard at work digging out the side of the mountain for the basement and building the cabin with a brick fireplace, a half loft, full basement, and a green tin roof using no power tools. The deck facing the creek ran twenty feet wide and ten feet deep. After I added a rectangular picnic table and benches and some rocking chairs, I practically lived on that deck. I love being outdoors.

Selling my rustic house on six acres in Woodstock, less than an hour south of Ellijay, provided me with the cash money for the lot, the log cabin package, and the labor to build the cabin. I had a little money left to get me through until I could land a job. After days of desperate searching, I was hired by an adolescent therapy program in Blue Ridge, Georgia, as a counselor working with adolescents with adjustment difficulties.

My divorce from Mark was complicated. He had swept me off

my feet with his thick Finnish accent, his charismatic personality, slender, muscular build, blue eyes, and long blonde hair. Now I was confused and scared, even though I was the one who had left the marriage. Our four-year relationship had been a whirlwind of excitement after meeting on a steamboat in New Orleans. Since he lived about five hours south of my home, we took turns commuting on weekends for a long time before getting married in a park, with wedding pictures of me in my dress seated behind him on his bright-yellow Harley. When I bought the house in Woodstock, he moved in with me and continued buying old cars and selling them to eager buyers in Finland, who loved old American cars. Then Finland increased import taxes, and Mark's business was no longer profitable. Mark had a plan to build sets in the movie and television business, but that transition took time and, in the meantime, he was bringing in less money.

Why did I get so angry that I just impulsively turned off our phone service? Why had I gotten so frustrated and impatient? Stressed to the max over money after leaving my job to start a business of my own, I was afraid I would lose the house. Driving back and forth from Woodstock to Douglasville to work had taken its toll. I was exhausted, mentally and physically. So, I struck out on my own and joined a counseling group closer to home, but it just took too long to get enough clients to pay the bills. I beat myself up for moving too fast. Now, fear overwhelmed me.

Mark and I had different lifestyles too. I went to bed early so I could get up and drive an hour in traffic to work, and I rarely got home before ten at night. Mark worked for himself, so his hours were flexible and he often stayed up late playing loud music while he worked on cars in the garage. The logistics of living under one roof didn't work. He was very extroverted and had a lot of company, and I needed quiet time. We loved each other, but it would have been better if we had continued to live apart. I even tried to get a permit to build another house on the six acres, but there wasn't enough land that could be approved for a septic tank. The inspector just said to me that it wouldn't "perk." So, one of my counselor friends bought the house and I found the Ellijay property after many hours on the phone.

Buying the steep Ellijay lot impulsively was a sort of break with reality, an action taken by a brain that was overloaded and a heart that was broken. Since breaking out on my own and having my own business, I had stayed up many nights worrying about money. Why I thought I could support myself in an even smaller town, I have no idea. I guess stress skewed my thinking.

My plan was to work as a licensed professional counselor (LPC) in some capacity and eventually start my own private practice. At that time, I had a master's degree in psychology and an LPC license that I had earned the year before. I would get a job to get money coming in quickly and then gradually open my own therapy practice in the evenings. Over a year or so, I hoped to expand my therapy practice to full time. Sick of attaching labels to people so that insurance would pay for therapy sessions, I planned to take the huge risk of having a self-pay business for adults who were willing to pay out of pocket. My idea was that the clients would be more motivated and I could now narrow my clientele to only adults.

That determination to be independent brought me back to the top of my steep driveway the next morning. Dressed to ride, I walked down the stairs to the basement, pushed up the kickstand, guided my motorcycle to the lip of the carport at the crest of the driveway, and swung into the seat. The driveway was still as impossibly steep as it was the day before and the curve still seemed too perilous to navigate.

But this time, after convincing myself the night before, I said to myself, "You are the only one here, just you and this motorcycle. You really want to ride, so do it." I imagined myself riding confidently down the long, winding dirt driveway, like I had visualized over and over the night before. I saw myself getting to the bottom of the driveway and then turning onto the dirt road that wound down the mountain until it merged with pavement at the entrance to the community. From there, I would be on level ground all the way to town.

My legs were shaking against the motorcycle. My hands were clammy inside my gloves. My heart was racing. I was so scared. But this time, I was focused on my goal. This time there was no turning back. So, I pushed the pedal into first gear. Then I let go of the brake and yelled at the top of my lungs, "I'm scared!" and hung on for dear life.

Chapter 1

Feeling Free

Months before my driveway escapade, I was eager to watch the cabin being built. "I've got an idea," I said to my son, Trey, and my stepdaughter, Sunny, ages nine and eleven. "Let's camp out across the creek and watch Sam and the guys build the cabin!" We had driven to Ellijay to see how the building was going on the Valley View Drive home. The basement of the cabin had been finished and the crew was bringing in the lumber and other materials to start the actual building. Trey and Sunny both chimed in, "Yes!" and that began our fun adventure. We sat on the ground and figured out what we would need for the next two weeks.

I had a light blue-and-gray dome tent that had provided fun shelter many times on camping trips to Florida and North Carolina. We would gather up sheets, blankets, pillows, towels, washcloths, and soap. Each of us had our clothes and toiletries. Other necessities like flashlights, trash bags, and an ice chest would be stored behind the back seat of my car. I made a note to buy a little hibachi grill for cooking dinners.

When we were all set, we walked across the creek to watch the guys putting up the exterior walls. Eventually, the roof, the loft, the interior walls, the electrical wiring, the plumbing, and the big fireplace with a hearth and mantle would be added. Sam and the guys made the kitchen cabinets themselves. I just had to choose a design for the front doors. I like simplicity, so I just asked for one diagonal board going across the front of vertical boards.

During the days, Trey and Sunny and I walked about a half a mile down the curved dirt road and took the turn to the swimming pool. The pool was big, not crowded, and well maintained. Many days, we went to the pool in the morning and the afternoon. My daughter Heather and her friends came up to swim that summer too. There was a building with toilets and sinks and also showers at the pool. So, when we went for our afternoon swim, we would bring clean clothes, and then we could shower and change before walking back to the cabin. When I think back, those showers made it possible for us to stay for two weeks.

When we went to town, though, we drove in my Wrangler, with the soft, convertible top and four-wheel-drive manual transmission. When Tom and I first drove in his car to see the Ellijay property, Tom replied to Sam's concern about the steep driveway, "Oh, she's got a Willys. She'll be fine." He was referring to Willys-Overland Motors, who created Jeep.

I had been told that Jimmy and Rosalynn Carter had a house just outside Walnut Mountain. One day on our way to lunch, after passing the security shack on our right, we saw Jimmy and Rosalynn walking toward the road, followed by a security detail. Jimmy smiled a great big friendly smile and waved, and we waved back. My daughter Laurie Grace, who was eighteen years old then, noticed that the security guys were dressed in casual shirts in a flowery, almost Hawaiian, style, and dark glasses. It was like they were trying to blend in as tourists or guests rather than wearing the typical Secret Service dark suits. They walked about ten feet behind Jimmy and Rosalynn, but the noticeable earpieces and phones gave them away.

We were headed to our favorite barbeque place, Poole's Barbeque, better known as Pigs on the Hill. Colonel Poole and his wife started their famous barbeque restaurant in a small building that was hard to notice from I-515. Not only was it a distance from the interstate, but there is a small road between the Colonel's establishment and the interstate. Anyway, the Colonel's request to have a big sign for advertising was rejected, so he ingeniously came up with the idea of wooden pig-shaped signs on the hill next to the restaurant. He said you could have your own pig for "five dollars and an honest face." When you paid the money, they put your name on the pig sign.

Hiking on the dirt roads and paths was like second nature on the mountain. I walked so many miles alone and with the children. On my first hike alone, I was trekking up a hill and I heard loud bird songs. There were so many birds singing and chattering that I thought for a minute that it was a recording piped in to set a "you're in the woods" tone. I quickly came to my senses and realized that the birds were real. I lived in the woods.

In Ellijay, the Ellijay River and the Cartecay River converged to make the Coosawattee River. River rafting was a very popular sport. In Blue Ridge, just twenty miles north of Ellijay on I-515, the Toccoa River attracted hundreds of campers each year. Rafting became a frequent weekend activity. I had loved camping since I was in my forties and decided to buy a tent. Laurie Grace and Trey and I camped a lot in North Carolina, and Heather would join us occasionally. I quickly grew to love the mountains. On the next trip, I planned to look at log cabins in North Georgia on the way to North Carolina. The children were patient and seemed to enjoy looking at all styles of log cabins in many different locations. It wasn't a stretch for me to build a log cabin in Ellijay.

I liked living in a log cabin in the mountains. According to my plan, I got a full-time job first. I was a mental health counselor at an outdoor therapeutic program for adolescents. I knew that I wanted to have my own therapy business as quickly as possible, and to do that I needed to make connections in the community. I also wanted to grow spiritually, so I began to read books and to meet others who were on the same path. I welcomed challenge and opportunities to learn. Freedom to me included no longer working in a job that clashed with my values, having the time to enjoy nature, following my life's purpose. Freedom was also riding my motorcycle. I had gotten my motorcycle license right before moving to Walnut Mountain so that I could ride where I wanted and when I wanted. In the next four years, I would ride everywhere, to work, to the grocery store, to get my hair done, to run errands, and I would sometimes ride long distances. That motorcycle represented freedom to me. When I rode, I felt free.

Chapter 2

Building a Community

After facing my fear and finally riding my motorcycle to the bottom of the precarious, steep driveway, I leaned left and turned my motorcycle onto Valley View Road, turned left up a hill, left again and then a right, and I was on the main road toward the Walnut Mountain entrance. I passed the short road to the swimming pool on my right and after many descending, winding curves, I arrived at the entrance and waved at the man in the guard house on the right. I felt more confident as I rode several miles on Turniptown Road before turning right toward the Ellijay square.

I rode with a rapidly running river to my left almost all the way to town. Passing through an intersection, I came to Apple A Day Health Food Store on my right. Since I wanted to start making connections, I pulled to the right and parked my motorcycle in the parking lot, hooked my helmet on the handlebars, and walked into the store. I was greeted by the owner, Louise Crawford, whom I soon learned was straightforward, knowledgeable, smart, and quick-witted. She also had a genuine interest in helping her patrons.

"Hi, I'm Louise. How can I help you?" she asked.

"Hi, I'm Laurie. I just moved to Ellijay and I haven't been in your store, so I thought I'd stop in."

"Welcome to Ellijay and to my store. Would you like to try some juice?"

Louise and I connected immediately and chatted for a long time before I left, assuring her that I would be back soon. I frequented the store and Louise and I became very good friends.

Pulling out of the driveway, I turned right and headed to the quaint Ellijay downtown square. There was a bed-and-breakfast on my right and as I turned right onto the square, there were mom-and-pop antique shops, a furniture store on the corner as I turned left, more local shops, and another antique store before I saw the library ahead. I stopped at the library, meeting an eccentric man who was well-known in town for riding his loaded-down bicycle everywhere even though he had designed and built an electric car with a battery life of ten miles to a charge. That day, he was in the library demonstrating how to construct wooden candlesticks. I was fascinated by this man, who was an innovative genius who lived simply while spending time creating and building his inventions. Ellijay, I soon learned, was a mecca for creative souls.

Next on my right was the courthouse, where the League of Women Voters held meetings. I joined the group because I believed that hearing the views of men and women running for various positions firsthand would help me get to the truth. I was curious about their values and what issues they considered important to tackle. I frankly do not remember any particular person who spoke, but I was inspired by those who seemed honest and passionate.

Ellijay had retained its historic past, not giving in to "progress" in the form of tall buildings or franchises as so many towns had. The zeal of a group of dedicated citizens in the Historical Society contributed to keeping the small-town feel in Ellijay. The charm of downtown Ellijay was that the businesses, including the restaurants, were locally owned and operated. That day as I rode into town, I decided to try Ruthie's Restaurant, which I had heard made delicious homemade pies. I grabbed a slice of coconut pie on my right as I walked in, then sat down to enjoy fried chicken, turnip greens, and cornbread. This café would become a meetup place occasionally as I made friends in the community.

On my way out of downtown Ellijay, I passed by Sailors Drive on my right, where I would soon have my first therapy office. With a bottling plant in my rearview mirror, I passed a grocery store, then headed south on I-515. My next destination was Panorama Farms, one of about twenty-five places to buy fresh local apples. My favorite were Yates apples, which were ready to be picked late in September or October. They were small, crisp, and tart. The parking lot was huge to accommodate the hundreds of visitors, both locals and tourists, who visited in the summer and fall. The aroma of freshly baked apple pies and breads permeated the air. "I'll take a loaf of apple bread, please," I said to the woman behind the counter. Jars of every kind of jam imaginable filled the shelves, and bins were teaming over with at least a dozen kinds of apples, plus other locally grown vegetables. You could even buy ice cream and fudge. I strung the bag with the bread and the bag of Yates apples over my handlebars and started the motorcycle. Pumpkins of all sizes were on my left as I pulled out of the parking lot, but I would wait until the weekend and bring my son, Trey, to pick out the soon-to-be jack-o'-lanterns.

Riding north on I-515, I pulled into the parking lot of a strip shopping center anchored by an Ingles grocery store. I noticed a small bookstore and at the end of the strip was the post office. Ellijay had everything I needed, including a movie theatre up Maddox Drive. Trey and Sunny and I had watched a couple of movies there in the summer. The ticket prices were much cheaper than in Woodstock and the popcorn and soft drinks were one dollar each.

Yes, I liked this small town. The people were open, friendly, and casual. I didn't have to drive a long distance for what I needed. The scenery was beautiful with the mountains, the rushing rivers, and the autumn leaves turning red, orange, and gold. This was a place where my unconventional style would be applauded. This community would welcome me with open arms and make me feel at home. I would be inspired to realize many of my dreams and a foundation would be developed for another, even more inspiring experience to come in Arizona. For now, I would focus my energy and time building a community here in Ellijay.

Chapter 3

Solitude

In the evenings, I was alone with nature and with my thoughts. The natural surroundings and the quiet provided just what I needed to begin to formulate ideas about the future. It had been fun to spend time tent camping and watching the cabin being built, but now that I was settled, it was time to spend time with myself figuring out how I was going to build a community and how I was going to move forward. One evening, I sat in a rocking chair on my big deck, looking out at the mountain ridge. Being outdoors with nature's beauty inspired me to think big thoughts.

I knew no one in Ellijay when I made the leap to move to a new town brimming with new adventures and many folks of various backgrounds, personalities, and interests. I really wanted connection with kindred spirits, people who liked to read, think, and explore ideas. I needed the mental stimulation and I also needed the support and encouragement of others. As I sat on the deck and looked out at the mountain range, I felt a settling calm, but I was also still struggling with confusion. The divorce from Mark, which I don't like to admit was my third divorce, was a wake-up call. My first husband had left me. I left the second marriage because I didn't feel understood for who I was apart from my roles as wife and mother. In this third marriage, I initiated the divorce from Mark because I knew that we were both discontented. He was chomping at the bit to go further with a career building sets for movies and television shows and really wanted to move close to Hollywood. I needed to make a job change, because I was exasperated with a job that didn't express my values.

This was a real turning point for me. I first told myself that I moved to Ellijay to get away from work that I didn't like and a marriage that wasn't letting either of us grow. What I wanted to figure out was what I was moving toward. "I have gotten lost somehow," I said out loud.

So, I turned inward. I spent time evaluating not just my situation, but myself. *Who am I really? What do I want from life? What do I really want to do?* I wrote my thoughts in a journal. I also wrote down my dreams. Ever since I studied Sigmund Freud and Carl Jung as part of my psychology major studies, I had been fascinated with the idea that dreams are the raw, uncensored data lodged in the unconscious. The theory is that when you remember your dreams, you can analyze the emotions, plot, and ending to learn more about your true self.

Ideas came to me in the solitude. What the quiet and Mother Nature provided was an environment where I could read and study and expose myself to new information and new ideas. I bought the Sacred Path Cards created by Jamie Sams, a member of the Wolf Clan Teaching Lodge. I was drawn to the cards because on the back cover was written, "This extraordinary tool for self-discovery draws on the strength and beauty of Native American spiritual tradition. Developed by Native American medicine teacher Jamie Sams, this unique system distills the essential wisdom of the sacred teachings of many tribal traditions and shows users the way to transform their lives."

This was before I used the internet, so there wasn't the option of just looking online and finding a relevant book to buy. I walked into the bookstore in Kennesaw, Georgia, and wandered into sections that interested me. Then I pulled books from the shelves and found a table in the coffee shop, where I looked at the front cover and read the back cover, then skimmed the inside as I enjoyed a cup of coffee. I loved browsing in a bookstore.

The Sacred Path Cards included a hardcover book that explained how to spread the cards and how each lesson pertained to me personally. Every day I sat on one of the two benches on either side of my picnic-style yellow pine kitchen table and got out the cards and the book. After shuffling the cards, I spread them out on the table. Trusting my intuition, I chose cards to make one of the various spreads. Then I took notes on the guidance about my strengths and weaknesses and possible courses of action that would further my personal and spiritual growth. *What is this teaching me? What direction do I go now?* I realized that the daily ritual was helpful in giving me guidance and bringing a structure to my pursuit of wisdom.

One day in the bookstore, I decided to walk to the New Age section in the back of the store. A young man who worked there eagerly offered assistance.

"I want to learn more about spirituality," I told him.

Immediately, he asked, "Have you read any of Carlos Castaneda's books?"

"No, I've never heard of Carlos Castaneda," I replied.

As I studied Jamie Sams's cards and book and read Castaneda's books, I quickly discovered that a crucial step for spiritual growth was reading and pondering the books that offered wisdom. I started reading about the experiential teachings of the wise Yaqui elder, Juan Matus, in the book *The Teaching of Don Juan: A Yaqui Way of Knowledge* (1968). I felt my way of thinking shift dramatically. Not just shift, but open up, like my consciousness just cracked open.

I resonated with Carlos, a graduate student in anthropology at UCLA. He took off for northern Mexico to learn about Native American cultural and spiritual beliefs from a Yaqui elder that he heard about, but hadn't even met. *That's something I would do*, I thought. Castaneda returned to northern Mexico many times over a period of years, because his curiosity drove him to learn more. I could so relate to him.

One of the lessons that Juan Matus taught Carlos was that if you want to catch rabbits, go where the rabbits are. I knew that I wanted to meet intelligent, interesting women who liked to read. *Where do I find them?* They are often in bookstores, coffee shops, and movie theatres, three of my favorite places. But, how do I cross paths with them? How do I find kindred spirits? I needed an idea.

Chapter 4

Kindred Spirits

I'll start a book discussion group. That was the idea that came into my mind. I had never participated in a book discussion group, much less started one. I knew I loved to read and I loved to talk about books. So, I took my intention to the local bookstore that I had seen in a strip shopping center on I-515 and talked with the owner. "I want to start a book discussion group and I thought your bookstore would be a great place. My plan is to meet once a month and discuss a different book. The group members would buy the book and read it before the meeting. We could buy all the books from you. So, you sell some books, and more people will be coming into your store."

"It's a good idea, but I don't have enough room," he explained. Next, I drove to the Corner Stone Café just on the other side of an antique store on a side street off the quaint Ellijay square where I had eaten lunch a few times. My favorite meal was French onion soup in a pastry bowl, served with crusty bread and butter. It was so delicious and I looked forward to enjoying the wonderful smell of the soup simmering as I walked in the door. Toward the back of the room there was a counter with stools where you could sit and eat. That's where I headed when I was by myself. I always hoped someone would hop up on another stool and then one of us would start a conversation.

In the main area, there were lots of rectangular wooden tables and chairs spaced out enough so that you didn't feel crowded. The front door was glass with a wooden frame painted glossy white. There was a double window to the right of the door and another double window centered to the left of the door with its white wooden casings that matched the door.

"I want to start a book discussion group and I'm looking for a place to meet," I explained to the owner.

She loved the idea of the book club meeting there, and asked, "Could the group meet after we close for the day? We stay another two hours or so to clean up. If everyone would just buy a cup of coffee or a dessert, then it would be worth it to me."

"Sounds great! Would you mind if I tape a flyer to the counter in front of your cash register and another one in the window to let people know about the meetings?" We agreed on the first Thursday of each month at 6:30 p.m. and away we went. That was the start of the book discussion group. I had no idea how many people would show up. I just posted the date and time for the first meeting on the flyers and hoped people would come.

About twelve women came to the first meeting, so we pushed a few tables together. I started the evening with, "Hi, I'm Laurie and I'm new to Ellijay, so I don't know any of you and I don't know if you know each other. How about we start by going around the table and introducing ourselves." Each woman gave her name and what kind of books she usually read. After some discussion about book genres that we had in common, we chose a book for the next meeting. The book discussion group was born. And, of course, it turned out that most of us were kindred spirits.

By kindred spirits, I meant open-minded readers who enjoyed thought-provoking books. In addition, kindred spirits wouldn't enjoy answering the structured questions posed by authors in the backs of some books. This book discussion group would have open discussions about motivations and intentions and deep meanings and layers of meaning. Often the book choices would be, to say the least, unusual.

An opportunity for interesting discussion came from a local

author who wrote about his fear that the polar icecaps were going to melt, causing the sea levels to rise and destroy coastlines. In the 1990s, researchers in the Arctic were noticing some floating ice as a result of melting. So, this theory was not unique to our local author, but his specific prediction of a date when this would turn into a catastrophe was unusual. He predicted that on 5-5-5, which, if I remember correctly, stood for May 5, 2005, major flooding would erode coastlines as a result of the polar cap melt. Most of the women were so interested in how he figured out a particular date that we all met at one of the women's homes and watched a video about his ideas. That led to some interesting discussion.

When the book *Second Sight* by Judith Orloff, MD, was published, I suggested to the group that we read it and I was delighted when everyone agreed. The book was nonfiction, which was my favorite genre. The first-time author was a traditionally trained psychiatrist who was also psychic. For example, she had premonitions about deaths and earthquakes. When handed a house key, without knowing whose key it was, she was able to describe the house exterior and interior in detail. She had also worked with the police to locate missing persons.

The women in the group felt completely comfortable expressing their opinions. We talked about our individual thoughts about psychics and about Judith Orloff, in particular. Her work combining her psychic gifts with her psychiatric therapy practice got a lot of mixed views. But most of us agreed that the author was interesting and her work was interesting, whether we completely believed her or agreed with her or not. That was the beauty of this group of women. They shared their different viewpoints and interpretations with each other without anyone needing to be "right." That's what was so fascinating. They shared various perspectives from their various life experiences. We had some thought-provoking conversations.

Not everyone who showed up felt as eager to read unconventional books. So, a person might come once, seem rather bewildered with our taste in books, and never be seen again. And, some gals preferred a more structured approach to discussing books, so one of the women formed another group. I love it when that happens. That's what makes life interesting—so many people with so many different preferences and interests. Whether they liked the unstructured discussion of unusual authors or the structured style of more conventional books, they were all lovers of books. They were also people who liked to connect, to gather together, with fellow readers. I knew the feeling of finishing a book that I absolutely loved to the point of obsession and feeling so let down when the book was over. And, the worst part was when there was no one to talk with about the book. The group connected kindred spirits to talk about books.

It reminded me of my experience of being in a theatre audience watching an intriguing movie. There might be times when everyone laughed or gasped or grew still. But, when the credits started, they all got up to leave. I did not understand it. When I was really involved in a movie that pulled me in, I stayed and watched the credits. I was interested in the filming locations and how many stuntmen or women there were and how many people it took to make the movie.

One time, I was watching an Adam Sandler movie and I was rewarded for my curiosity about the making of the movie. I can't remember the name of the movie, but I do remember that *after* the credits, Adam had added a tribute to his dad. It was very touching. I cried, sitting alone in the theatre, while the clean-up crew disposed of empty popcorn containers, candy boxes, and soda cups. Only those of us across the country who were the patient watchers of credits were rewarded with the surprise of a usually funny actor taking the time to remember and pay tribute to someone he loved.

I wondered if there were statistics on the percentage of moviegoers who stayed for the credits. I have enjoyed the company of other people watching the credits on rare occasions. Then I thought, *These are kindred spirits.* And I soaked up those moments when I felt connected to other human beings.

After watching the 1996 movie *The Chamber*, based on a book by John Grisham, I literally could not move to leave. The agenda of the author, which was evident in the film, was that the death penalty should be abolished because sometimes innocent people are killed for crimes that they did not commit. The last scene, where the woman is desperately running with evidence that would save the convicted man but gets there too late, tied me up in knots. Not only was I unable to move, I also could not speak. It was quite a while after my friend and I drove out of the parking lot that I could find words to talk about my riveting experience.

Years before, in the early 1980s, my mother was reminded of my focused attention when reading books as she tried to get my attention to ask a question. She and I had flown to New Haven, Connecticut, to prepare an apartment for her older sister, my Auntie Grace, after she finally resigned herself to the fact that she could no longer live in the family home with its stairs and maintenance. Auntie Grace moved into an apartment in town where she could also use public transportation, since she could no longer drive. After a long day of making decisions about furniture and what went where, I was glad to lose myself in a biography of Dolly Parton. Mother later told me that she attempted repeatedly to get my attention, but my undivided focus was on the book. Dolly's story fascinated me because she knew who she was and what she wanted to do with her life at a very early age. She was fascinated with the fancy clothes and makeup of the prostitutes in town and quickly went to work creating her new image. Her creativity also manifested in songwriting, beginning with simple stories of her family and her experiences growing up. Being born into a family who played musical instruments and sang was an obvious influence. Dolly chose to share her talent with the world and to manifest her dedication to education by buying books for children. She was making a difference. That's what hooked me.

Meeting so many kindred spirits in the book discussion group gave me the courage to start planning for my own therapy practice. I no longer wanted a counseling practice under the direction of someone else or a practice within a limited liability business agreement, like the one I had in Woodstock, Georgia. Even though getting referrals from insurance companies and employee assistance programs made it easier to build up a business, I wanted to have a self-pay business. I decided that I would not take insurance.

My thinking was that when people pay out of pocket, they would be more motivated in their path to self-discovery. I also didn't want to hire anyone to handle insurance. But the main reason was my belief that therapy was about more than eradicating symptoms. Therapy includes an exploration of who you are and what you believe about yourself and about life, in general.

For example, I wouldn't ask a client, "Do you believe in God?" Instead, I would frame it like this: "What is your concept of God?" One of the most interesting responses to that question came from a woman who very matter-of-factly responded, "Colors." That unusual reply gave me some rich material that would help me get to know her on a deeper level. I realized that I got the most satisfaction from working with adults because I could delve into Albert Ellis's theory that your beliefs lead to your thoughts that lead to your feelings that lead to your behavior. I started with beliefs. I was very curious about the beliefs that led to the response "Colors."

I decided to put my intention to find some office space out into the universe and see what happened. This was another life lesson from the spiritual books that I was reading and the Sacred Path Cards that I was interpreting for further guidance. Days later, an interesting voice mail was on my phone. I can vividly remember coming in from work and seeing the red button blinking on the phone. This was before cell phones, so I had gone all day without having a personal phone call or getting a personal message.

The voice on the phone said, "Hi, Laurie. This is Marion McCumber. Three different people have mentioned your name to me this week, so I think it's a sign that I should call and offer you some office space." Immediately, I knew that Marion and I were kindred spirits because she said, "I think it's a sign." I knew that she was spiritual and that she heeded signs when she made decisions. She knew that signs could be events that alerted her to what was truth or they could prompt her to take action. She interpreted the phone calls as a sign, not a coincidence.

I couldn't call her back fast enough! We arranged a time to meet at her office. The office buildings were at the end of Sailor Drive, so it was an easy drive for me. I just took the road that I would travel to the Ellijay square and turned left at the bottling plant. There were eight offices in an "L" shape, all dark-brown wood with gray roofs. Each building had two office suites with a rock wall making the distinction between the separate doors and stairs. Each suite had a set of eight wooden steps and a big wooden handrail leading to the front landing and glass door. The door casings were painted red.

Marion greeted me in the waiting room with an upbeat, "Hi, Laurie. I'm glad to meet you." Marion had an easygoing demeanor, which was reflected in her casual dress. She was a massage therapist who was renting an office suite with a waiting room, two office rooms, and a bathroom. One of the office rooms held her massage table, a small wooden table for her oils, homeopathic remedies, and a compact disc player, a chair for clients to sit and change clothes, and paintings on the wall. She wasn't using the other room, so she had decided to rent it.

After I had the tour and we got acquainted, she offered me the room for a therapy office for two hundred dollars a month, a very reasonable amount. That was important to me because I was only going to charge sixty dollars an hour for therapy and I would be starting with zero clients. Even after I put the word out, it would take time to build a practice. And, initially I would see clients after my full-time job hours.

My office furnishings consisted of a red, blue, and green plaid love seat, side tables, a chair, a floor lamp, a candle, and a box of tissues. Also, I kept a file chest so that I could lock up the handwritten clients' charts and keep the initial forms organized and on file. I didn't use a computer for my business, so I didn't really need a desk. I had a clipboard and pens for the clients to complete forms, like basic information and confidentiality consent forms. A hardcover notebook that I held in my lap to take notes during sessions was on a side table.

Marion didn't have a receptionist and I didn't need one, either. When it was time to meet with a client, I just walked out into the waiting room, greeted them, and walked with them to the office. For privacy, I scheduled clients far enough apart that they didn't see each other coming and going. In other words, one client would have left the building and driven away before another arrived. That's another way that I did things differently from most therapy practices, where there is a fifty-minute session and a ten-minute break in between. My style was to meet with a client for an hour and leave a thirty-minute break to write up my notes, including ideas for the next session. I also had plenty of time for a bathroom and refreshment break.

To attract people to my practice, I started by offering a one-night "How to Be Healthy" session. A few women came and the talk soon turned to the importance of exercise for emotional and physical health. Out of that, the idea for a hiking group evolved. Ellijay was full of hiking trails, some more rigorous than others. On Saturday mornings, we met at various trails that we found in a "hiking trails of Georgia"-type book.

On one hike, our group of six women got lost after we had walked an hour or so. The trail was not well marked and we apparently made a wrong turn. After searching for the trail that would lead us back to our cars, we heard the sound of cars. Relief! We followed the sound until we came to the parking lot. Most of the time, though, we enjoyed relaxing walks on narrow dirt trails, talking about the various plants and the beauty of a river flowing. Each woman brought water and snacks, so sometimes we took a break along the water before continuing our hike. A few of the women who joined the hiking group also became my clients.

Another way I networked was face-to-face meetings with

people in the community. I made appointments with local medical doctors to introduce myself and explain how mental health issues, for example, stress, affected physical health. In those days and in this rural community, doctors were glad to take some time to meet me and learn about my services. I left them with some business cards and a promise to reciprocate by recommending their services to my clients.

Marion and I worked well together in that Sailor Drive office. Everything seemed to just flow seamlessly. We truly were kindred spirits. I believed, as she did, that we were brought together for a reason. We both wanted to help people, to nurture, encourage, and guide them. Our goal was not to get rich, but just to be able to make enough money to pay the bills with a little cushion left over. We were both one-woman businesses, making our own appointments, meeting clients, and serving the community.

Then, one day, Marion informed me that she was going to move to a big house on a hill closer to the square. Her plan was to live there and work there. I went to see her new house and talk about the logistics of moving my office to her new residence/office. As I entered the big white two-story house there was a sign outside that said something like, "Whatever you believe is your reality." Another example of how Marion and I had similar beliefs.

The house needed some TLC, some painting, but no major repairs were needed. At this point, Marion had already purchased the house with a nice front yard. I really liked her idea of living upstairs and working downstairs. This way, she could afford a bigger home, since she wouldn't be paying extra for office rent. The problem was that she now wanted four hundred dollars a month for my portion. I still had a very small business and the idea of being obligated to that much money each month made me feel overwhelmed. So, I had to say, "Marion, I really like your idea and I'm so happy for you. But I just don't feel comfortable committing to four hundred dollars a month."

So, the kindred spirits flew in different directions, but we still chatted on the phone and met occasionally. Once, she called because she was experiencing some emotional distress. We met for a long lunch and worked through her issues. She gave me a free massage once when I was particularly stressed. Marion was a kindred spirit who provided an opportunity to have my own therapy practice.

CHAPTER 5

OFF THE BEATEN PATH

Not being one to approach life tasks in conventional ways, I often traveled off the beaten path when it came to getting continuing education units (CEUs) to maintain my licensed professional counselor license. While I sometimes drove from Ellijay to Atlanta to take classes from my counselor friend, Karen McCleskey, which were interesting and informative, I also drove long distances if a workshop topic interested me.

During the time that I was still sharing office space with Marion, I decided to drive to Valdosta, Georgia, a five-hour drive, because the theme was Native American culture. I had been fascinated with Native Americans for years. I took Heather, Laurie Grace, and Trey camping at the KOA in Cherokee, North Carolina, many times. I liked the idea of the Cherokee Indians getting money from at least some of the stores that sold Native American wares in town. We also went on an educational tour at the Cherokee Village set up to demonstrate the many skills of the Cherokee, including making canoes, sculpting pottery, weaving baskets, and designing beadwork. They also made and demonstrated blowguns used to kill birds and small animals.

We spent an evening watching the outdoor drama *Unto These Hills*, which depicts the sad journey of the Cherokee on the Trail of Tears. What we learned was that some of the Cherokee escaped into the Blue Ridge Mountains, and their lineage still live there today. But, horrifically, most of the Cherokee, women and children included, were forced to walk the long, arduous trail to Oklahoma. Their removal allowed the white settlers to claim the gold and other resources so bountiful in North Carolina. To make the drama more intense, they shot real black-powder weapons, which were really loud.

I also took the children to the Native American Festival and Mother's Day Powwow in Canton, Georgia. The Cherokee elders explained their reverence for mothers as they celebrated through singing, drumming, and dancing. Trey and I joined the dancers in a circle dance, moving our feet to the beat of the drums. There were also Aztec dancers and a hoop dancer. Some of the dancers were competing for best in a particular style of dancing, including some very young children.

The costumes were brightly colored and some dancers wore bells on their ankles and others simulated birds while holding big feathers. The well-known performer Cherokee Rose sang many songs and was gracious enough to pose for pictures. The food, including corn on the cob served with lemon pepper, was served at many outdoor booths, and it was all delicious. Our fun find was fried alligator with fry bread. And the lemonade was the real deal, made from fresh-squeezed lemons. The outer perimeter was ringed with bales of hay for the audience to sit on.

Between events, we browsed the booths featuring dozens of artisans with their jewelry, flutes, clothing, artwork, and many other creations. There was a demonstration by a real alligator wrestler, who opened and closed the alligator's mouth and handled the alligator as if he had no fear whatsoever. Some of the Native Americans rode bareback on painted horses and stopped to chat with us. I grabbed at any opportunity to meet and interact with a Native person. Even though I have no Native American blood, I feel a strong kinship to these people who live close to Mother Earth, are so skilled at their crafts, and live their spiritual beliefs with everything they do.

So, when I got a flyer in the mail about a workshop on Native

American culture, I immediately sent in the registration fee. The workshop was being held at Valdosta State University, where classes on Native American studies were also offered to students. I parked in a parking space close to the designated building, and found the meeting with no problem. Immediately, I knew that I had made a good decision. The room was arranged in a big circle, and the presenter, a middle-aged Native American man, had obviously taken a lot of time to prepare a space that highlighted the four directions and Native American artifacts. I observed that he had taken much care in the handling and placement of the sacred objects.

North, South, East, and West, the four directions that carry great significance in the Native American belief system, were clearly designated. As soon as the presenter began to speak, I was in awe of his sincerity, and as he continued to share his beliefs, I realized that he had an incredible amount of knowledge and wisdom. I was mostly spellbound by the meanings that were attached not only to the four directions, but to each artifact.

Two questions that I often asked were (1) "What is the meaning of that?" and (2) "Why?" In our time together, the Native American presenter explained that every direction, every artifact, every detail in what he was wearing had meaning. I felt an instant connection with him and what he was demonstrating. Very careful thought was given to every aspect of his life, from the importance of the direction, East, for example, to the designs on his clothing. In other words, clothing details were not added merely because they added to the attractiveness of what he wore, but because they had meaningful significance.

"East," he explained, "is the direction where the sun comes up. The sun brings light." It is the beginning of a new day and each person's understanding of what they are being guided to accomplish is enhanced by light. Traditional people rise at dawn and face east, asking The Creator for wisdom and guidance throughout the day. You may have heard the term "to shed light on it," which means to have a better understanding of a particular subject. The same applies here. The sun's light spreads over the earth, illuminating everything in its path.

My observation was that in this Native American's life, he was fully present, fully conscious of every object and its meaning. He had certain artifacts for certain reasons. They were sacred, like their land is sacred or burial grounds are sacred. The depth of thought given to the inherent meanings resonated with me. The fact that he lived thoughtfully, fully conscious of the reason why he looked to a certain direction for guidance, why he wore a certain design, why he had certain beliefs, was a significant concept for me.

I didn't know then that a few years after attending this workshop I would actually work as a counselor on the Hopi Reservation in Arizona. Perhaps this face-to-face workshop and demonstration of Native American culture and spiritual beliefs was a step forward in my own spiritual journey. Certainly, a seed was planted, which would continue to grow with each book I read and each interaction I had with Native Americans. I felt drawn to their culture and to their spiritual beliefs, which included their perception of Mother Earth as a sacred nurturer. He shared his feeling of obligation to care for Mother Earth and to continue the cycle of creation.

When the presentation drew to a close, I stayed to meet the presenter and the sponsors who had made the workshop possible. I wanted to tell them how much I had learned and how inspired I was. I knew that it had taken a lot of time and energy to coordinate a workshop as well done as this one, and saying thank you was important to me.

I introduced myself to David Busch, PhD, who was a professor at Valdosta State University and had coordinated the event. I told David that I had driven all the way from Ellijay, Georgia, and I had learned so much that it was well worth the drive. David looked at me in surprise and told me that he and his family were moving to Ellijay. Who would have thought that I would drive five hours to meet someone who was planning to move to Ellijay?

Life can be so serendipitous and so interesting. David told me that he planned to open a private therapy practice there. His wife and children would join him in Ellijay as soon as he found office space and a place to live. We exchanged phone numbers and I told him that there was office space available next to mine that he might consider.

Not long after that, David leased the office space in the same group of office buildings and opened up his business. On the day that his wife, Cara, and the children drove up in the office suites parking lot, I joined David in welcoming them to Ellijay. Cara worked in his office, so I saw her and David frequently. Later, I would ask David to present at a Licensed Professional Counselors Association conference in Toccoa, Georgia, that I coordinated as the LPCA Northern District chairperson.

Traveling off the beaten path to Valdosta was an exhilarating experience. The workshop was thought-provoking and became another in a series of experiences and events that added to my knowledge of Native American culture. What I learned also added to my thirst for learning more about Native American spiritual beliefs, a curiosity that motivated me a couple of years later to travel over 1,700 miles to Flagstaff, Arizona, where I would live while I worked with the wonderful Hopi people. How often would it happen that I would drive to a meeting over three hundred miles from home and meet someone who had already planned to move to Ellijay? What are the chances of that happening? I often say, "You never know what's around the next bend." Veering off the conventional route can be full of surprises, seeing new places and meeting new people. Sometimes, getting off the beaten path can be a catalyst for change, like my decision to leave Ellijay and spend time in Arizona working as a counselor with the Hopis.

While I lived in Ellijay, Savannah was the destination for my next trip, this time to the Licensed Professional Counselors Association Annual Conference. There was nothing unconventional about attending the annual conference. I went every year, no matter where it was. Yes, I could earn many of the mandated CEUs for my license, but it was also an opportunity to spend some time with my counselor colleagues from all over the state of Georgia.

My maverick tendencies on this trip were reflected in my choice to sleep in my tent instead of sleeping in a comfy hotel room where the conference was being held. When I arrived in the outskirts of Savannah, I started looking for a campground. I had already done some research, so I knew there were many campgrounds surrounding Savannah. I decided to wait and pick one that I would like using my intuition. Kind of like "I'll know it when I see it" kind of thinking. Sure enough, as I approached Savannah on I-16, a sign for a locally owned and operated campground caught my attention. When I pulled in, I noticed that there were not many campsites and they were all for tent camping. My kind of place. I went in the office and found that it really was a mom-and-pop operation. The rate per night was reasonable and the couple who owned it was friendly. I picked out a site and pitched my tent for the two-night stay.

Why did I decide to go to the trouble of pitching my tent and driving each day from the campsite to the conference location? It didn't occur to me to take a course of action just to be different. My reasons for taking unbeaten paths vary from having an interesting experience to learning something new to doing something I have never done before to adding excitement to my life. In the case of sleeping in a tent in Savannah, I had a very definite reason. I had been experiencing some anxiety about when to break away entirely from working full time during the day and seeing clients in the evenings to quitting my full-time job and expanding my private practice to full time. I was getting emotionally weary from the long hours of therapy. But keeping the checkbook balanced was a big concern. I knew that sleeping close to the ground near the heartbeat of Mother Earth would get my mind, body, and spirit back in balance. Even though my friend Sonia offered to share her hotel bed with me so I wouldn't have to drive to the campground after the first day's events, I told her, "Thanks, but I really need to sleep in my tent."

What I didn't realize was that I also needed to just relax around a campfire. When I returned to the campground, a couple of guys at the adjoining site invited me over to sit by their fire. The fire was blazing, the beer was cold, and they were wonderful company. An interesting and low-key couple, they enjoyed being outdoors with a campfire and they provided stimulating conversation. Getting to know them and spending time with them was one of the highlights of my trip and definitely good for my soul.

The keynote speaker at the conference was the author Thomas Moore, whose 1994 book, *Care of the Soul: A Guide for Cultivating Depth and Sacredness in Everyday Life,* had been a best seller. I have to be honest, though, and tell you that he was not a hit with many of the counselors who didn't see the relevance of spirituality in therapy. I had been inspired by reading *Care of the Soul* and I thoroughly enjoyed his presentation, especially the discussion of using dreams in therapy. One of his questions to the audience was, "How many of you are flyers?" I raised my hand along with a few others. What he meant was how many of you see yourself flying in your dreams. I had dreams of flying frequently. Sometimes, I was flying an airplane. Sometimes I was flying on my own.

When he asked about flying dreams, I thought of a recurring dream I had been having recently. I was at an airport, getting ready to take off in a small plane. For some reason, there were barriers on either side of the runway, so when I taxied by them, the wings of the plane would hit them and get knocked off. I kept going, but I couldn't get off the ground. When I think of it now, the meaning of the dream seems obvious. I kept trying "to get off the ground" with my business and work independently, but the money issue kept holding me back. Sometimes I dreamed about flying without a plane, just holding out my arms and flying. I love that feeling of being free and flying completely unfettered. Just flying high above the ground and looking down without a care in the world seemed the ultimate freedom.

During the question-and-answer session, one of the women asked Thomas Moore if he would review manuscripts. I was pleasantly surprised when he said, "Yes, if it is an honest story." Over ten years later, I sent my rough draft of my book *Silent Decision* to him and asked for a critique. I was the psychology department chair at Barton College in Wilson, North Carolina, at the time and was casually checking my emails one afternoon, when I got his response with specific suggestions. Thank you, Thomas!

Those of us kindred spirits who found meaning in Thomas Moore's words tended to clique off and spend time together during meals. Sometimes we gathered in the hospitality suite, which was a hotel room rented for conference attendees to have social time together. One night, someone had the idea to have an experiential exercise to demonstrate the seven chakras. This was completely new to me. One of the guys agreed to lie on the floor and another person held a metal ring connected to a long string about six to eight inches over the person's body. I didn't know much about it then, but I quickly understood that the seven chakras, which start at the crown of your head and go to the bottom of the trunk of your body, are like swirling vortices of energy that correspond to nerves and organs in the human body. You may be familiar with them if you have studied yoga, meditation, or Eastern philosophies. It is best if the chakras are open so the energy rotates freely.

When it was my turn, the suspended ring moved a bit over the crown of my head. But when it was held over my forehead, between my eyes, the metal ring started to rotate on its own and soon it was swinging wildly in a circular motion. What surprised me was that several people laughed and didn't seem to be surprised. My elementary understanding of the forehead chakra had to do with intellectual thinking and intuition. People have remarked to me, "You think about everything, don't you, Laurie?" I guess they knew me better than I knew myself. Each time that I have had a reiki session, the reiki master worked to move some energy from my head and spread it throughout my body. That seemed to validate the ring swinging over my forehead.

At the conference the next day, I was looking at the books spread out on tables for sale, when I was approached by a young woman who obviously recognized me. She caught my attention with, "Laurie, my brother was one of your clients at Powers Ferry Adolescent Center in Marietta."

She told me his name and I immediately said, "Oh, yes! How is he doing?" She went on to tell me that he was doing really well, was focused and spending his time constructively, and was in college with a definite career in mind. When I worked at this residential facility for teens who had gotten off course with drugs or emotional upheavals, there were a couple of young men that I jogged with as we talked. For males, sitting face to face can feel confrontational and they sometimes clammed up. So walking or jogging side by side looking ahead and not at each other could help ease their anxiety so that they could relax and share what was on their mind.

This young man was very bright and he had entertained nontraditional kinds of spiritual and philosophical ideas in his mind. We had fascinating conversations about topics that, frankly, many counselors would have had a judgment about. I have always been very open-minded, so I could listen to his thoughts without feeling a need to censure or fix or judge. In response, he could open up, knowing that I was going to respond with interest in an effort to understand, not condemn.

Even with the jogging, I don't always click with a client and they don't always connect with me. This young man and I connected, and we jogged along while a myriad of ideas and thoughts flew back and forth between us. We were able to relate to each other in our common quest to make sense of all the different ways to view the energies and powers that can influence us throughout life. I was so glad to hear from his sister that our conversations built up his self-esteem and helped him move forward with his life. It's sort of like he was able to transition his thinking to "I'm okay even if I think of ideas that most people don't think or talk about."

I thought that because I chose to sleep in a tent and be close to Mother Earth, I was receptive and open, which contributed to crossing paths with my client's sister to learn that I had made a difference in his life. This was self-affirming since I was at a crossroads about moving forward with a full-time therapy practice and focusing more on starting a women's talking circle. Getting aligned with the heartbeat of Mother Earth also shifted some of my energy out of my head and into my heart. You know the popular phrase "Follow the path of heart" or "Follow your heart." If I followed my heart and did what I really wanted to do, I would focus solely on seeing clients and facilitating the women's group. My full-time job was not what I wanted to continue to do.

It was like a sign . . .

***

"I think I'm going to ride my motorcycle to a counselor workshop in Memphis," I said to my motorcycle buddy, JR. I mentioned this to JR after receiving a notice for a class that offered six CEUs with hypnotherapy as the topic, and an opportunity to get certified with additional hours. I continued, "It would be fun. I've never ridden that far on my own motorcycle. It would be an adventure."

JR was a motorcycle enthusiast, so he understood my motivation, but he cautioned me, "Laurie, there is no way that I am going to let you ride over four hundred miles by yourself to Memphis. There are too many things that could go wrong. I'm riding with you." JR was like an older brother to me, and he was the kind of person who enjoyed helping people.

I had met JR at a gas station in Jasper, Georgia, when I had stopped to put gas in my motorcycle. He was pumping gas into his motorcycle at the next pump, so we started to talk. The conversation started with small talk and then JR said, "Why don't we ride together some time?" and we exchanged phone numbers. I had been riding alone to run errands, shop at the grocery store, and to work. My full-time job then was in Jasper, Georgia, at the

Georgia Highlands Center, which provided seniors with physical and mental health services.

JR and I rode lots of places just for fun. One day, for example, I had Trey on the back of my motorcycle and we rode to Carters Lake and stopped to look at the dam. I remember that there were a couple of people fishing, and Trey was distressed that we hadn't brought fishing poles. JR also helped me by shortening the chain on my motorcycle by removing a link when it would get too slack. In other words, JR was a good friend. I learned that he had a construction business and that he took care of his mother, who lived close to him. And, I am so sad to add, years before I met him, his wife and child had been killed when their house caught fire. JR had been at work, and the firefighters were unable to rescue his family.

I saw JR as a responsible man and I also enjoyed his company, so when he proposed accompanying me to Memphis, I quickly said, "Great! That would be even more fun!" His suggestion was to leave the afternoon before my Saturday workshop. On our way out of town on that Friday, we drove our motorcycles to his job site so he could pay his crew for their week's work. Then we were on our way. Since it was almost four hundred miles, we didn't arrive in Memphis until about ten o'clock that night.

It's funny what stands out in my mind about that trip. When there weren't cars around, JR would sidle his motorcycle next to mine and reach out with a hard peppermint candy in his hand. I would laugh and grab the candy and then we would get back in formation. When you ride a motorcycle with someone, the rule of the road is to stay in the same lane, and to position yourselves diagonally so one of you is just ahead of the other. When JR brought me candy, he motioned and got beside me for the exchange.

When we got close to Memphis, there was a lot of road construction and a lot of riding over unfinished surfaces with grooves in them, so I had to concentrate to keep the motorcycle under control. We were warned in the motorcycle-training class about the possible dangers of riding over just this kind of road surface. We stopped for a dinner break, and then kept riding until we got to the campground. I had made a reservation ahead in this case, since we were arriving after dark and I needed to get an early start in the morning. We pitched the tent and headed to the showers before crashing for the night.

The next morning, we got up early, took down the tent, and packed our belongings in our saddlebags. My black leather saddlebags had plenty of room for my clothes and toiletries. I tied the tent onto the back of my seat so it jutted out to either side of the motorcycle. The plan was for me to ride to the workshop and JR would meet me later at the workshop site. Instead of riding directly back to Ellijay, JR suggested that we ride to Mobile, Alabama. "Let's make it a full weekend and go look at the shipyard before heading back to Ellijay Sunday afternoon. What do you think?"

I quickly responded, "Yes, why not?"

Before we got on the road, JR led me to a seafood restaurant on the Mississippi River. To get to it, we had to ride over big cobblestones, which were a bit tricky to negotiate. I love a challenge, so holding the handlebars tightly and weaving through the grooves just added to the thrill. JR informed me that he had worked in this area years before, so he knew about this restaurant that was built above the water, with a wooden walkway leading to the entrance. There was fresh fish, which I really like, and a wonderful view of the river while we ate. Here again, it's funny what you remember and what you don't when you attempt to dredge up details of the past. I cannot remember the name of the restaurant or exactly where it was located, except that it overlooked the massive Mississippi River. I remember the fresh fried trout that I enjoyed with coleslaw and hush puppies, though.

Frankly, part of the six-hour ride from Memphis to Mobile was miserable because we encountered rain. Neither of us wore a full helmet with a face shield, preferring to wear just a helmet and sunglasses, which also met safety regulations. The pelting rain felt like pins sticking my face. I kept hoping for the rain to quit so riding would be fun again. Sure enough, before we arrived in Mobile, the clouds parted and the sun came out, and we had an interesting and enjoyable time looking around at the shipyard. I recently found a photo of me sitting on my motorcycle with a big ship in the background.

The ride back to Ellijay was another six-hour ride from Mobile. I had a great trip combining work and pleasure. I also remember vividly that I quickly figured out that hypnosis was not for me. First of all, the six-hour workshop seemed like sixteen hours because I was really bored. Most important, I realized that I really was not interested in doing something to my clients, like hypnotizing them. What I was passionate about was the interchange of thoughts and ideas that transpired in a therapy session. Listening to a client's story and figuring out what was really going on that was contributing to their confusion, depression, or anxiety was really interesting to me. Then, creating a plan full of strategies that the client can use to facilitate change was meaningful to me because the client was empowered. The client and I brainstormed ideas, and then the client was in control of choosing to change their thinking patterns or not, reading a book I suggested or not, taking actions that we put on the table or not. They were in the driver's seat. Empowering clients to change their life was my goal.

So, I got my CEUs for the class, but that was the end of any interest in hypnosis. I had no regrets about the trip, though. Cruising along the highway on my motorcycle enjoying all the sights was great fun and I was mesmerized by the huge Mobile shipyard, where so much importing and exporting took place.

Just the feeling of freedom riding a motorcycle on a long trip was exhilarating for me. If I had just done the expected and driven to the class, just to learn that I didn't care one bit about adding hypnosis to my therapy skills, it probably would have been a bummer trip. I probably would have been aggravated that I went so far for a workshop that was not interesting to me, and had to put up with road construction while using up a lot of gasoline.

Riding the motorcycle and adding sightseeing in Mobile made it a fun and memorable experience. When JR and I stopped our motorcycles and looked out at all the ships, I exclaimed, "I had no idea there were so many big ships here. Wow, this is a real surprise. Mobile is a busy port, isn't it?"

"That's why I wanted you to see it, Laurie. I knew you would enjoy this experience."

"You got that right," I said. My motorcycle also got fifty miles to the gallon, so my travel expense was a lot less than driving a car. Yes, the practical aspect was not my main motivation. Just saying . . .

Another exhilarating experience from riding off the beaten path was my weekend trek to Suches. The curving road to Suches has been recognized by Rand McNally as a motorcyclist's dream route. I had read about the road, but my mission was to spend a night tent camping at Two Wheels Only, a campground exclusively for motorcyclists. This was an experience that I wanted so badly that I took off on a Saturday morning knowing that my motorcycle would not start unless I ran along beside it and then jumped on and kicked it in gear. No problem getting it to start at the bottom of my steep driveway, because I just rode it down, then kicked it into first gear at the bottom of the driveway. What I forgot was that I had to stop for gas, so I had no hill to ride down. When I finished filling the tank at the gas station, I just ran along beside the motorcycle, jumped in the seat, kicked it in gear, and away I went on my way to Suches.

I saw the sign Two Wheels Only on my left and pulled into a big parking lot in front of a lodge-style building with a wraparound porch. After parking my motorcycle, I walked into the building, passing several women sitting in wooden chairs on the porch. After signing in and paying to camp, I asked the manager, "Where can I set up my tent?"

He replied with a friendly smile, "Anywhere you find a place. It's first come, first serve."

Even though many tents were set up or being set up by fellow campers, I easily found a space and set up my blue-and-green tent. The spaces allotted for each tent on the grassy campground were large, so I had privacy, while being among fellow campers. Then, I went back to my motorcycle and got what I needed out of my saddlebags, and threw it in the tent after I had put down a sheet, pillow, and blanket. No blow-up mattress for me. I like being close to the earth.

The most fun part of the Suches camping experience was dinner. One of the options was to pay for a steak and grill it yourself on a big rectangular grill along with your fellow campers. That way, you got a steak grilled the way you liked it and you met people who were also cooking on the same grill. This was such a casual way to meet new people. I felt right at home at Two Wheels Only, where everyone there rode a motorcycle. You automatically have a connection. After I cooked my steak medium rare, I took my plate inside, where I added a baked potato and salad, then found a place to sit. The large room had lots of picnic type tables and benches for sitting. I was sitting at a table with three other people, and conversation was easy and relaxed.

After a satisfying meal and a busy day, I was eager to stroll around the campsites, stopping to chat at campfires. Campers, whether they ride motorcycles or not, are usually friendly and eager to invite you to join them around their fire. I had started camping only a few years before, when I decided to buy a tent and take the children camping. My parents didn't tent camp. When Daddy and Mother and I went on vacation to the ocean, we stayed in a cabin a short distance from the beach. Tent camping was my idea. After the first camping experience, I was hooked. I love being out in nature and sleeping under the stars. The night sounds of insects and frogs have their own soothing rhythm. Add to that the heartbeat of Mother Earth and I feel a real sense of tranquility. My mind gets in sync with the natural sounds and my body follows. I often take a long time to fall asleep wherever I am, but I enjoy a deeper sleep in a tent.

The next morning, I took my belongings out of the tent, took my tent down, and headed to the parking lot. As I approached my motorcycle and set down my stuff, I noticed a tall man working on his motorcycle. He looked up and said, "Hi!" which I interpreted as an invitation to introduce myself.

"Hi! My name's Laurie. What's yours?"

Dean, I learned, was doing some minor repair on his motorcycle, which got me thinking about the starting problem with my motorcycle. "My motorcycle won't start unless I run beside it and kick it in gear. Got any ideas?"

"Let me have a look," he smiled.

A very short time later, Dean had fixed the problem. We chatted a while and decided to ride together some time even though he lived in Chattanooga, Tennessee, and I lived in Ellijay, Georgia. We exchanged phone numbers, and went our separate ways.

Dean and I became friends. After several phone conversations, we rode together once and another time we went camping along a river. I learned that his dream was to have a laundromat/motorcycle repair shop combination. He found a buyer for my motorcycle a couple of years later, so I pulled it in a trailer to Chattanooga. He was a good friend. A few years after that, when I returned from Arizona, I rode the motorcycle that I bought there to a restaurant halfway between Chattanooga and Dawsonville, Georgia, where I lived then, to have dinner with Dean and his girlfriend. It was so cold that night that Dean loaned me a heated vest for my chilly ride home. I would have been miserable without it. Getting off the beaten path had brought many kindred spirits and good friends into my life.

Walking off the beaten path has also led to many epiphanies too. While hiking through Walnut Mountain one evening, I came upon an old brick chimney, apparently all that remained of a house long since gone. I felt a strong energy as I walked past and backed up to figure out its source. *I wonder if I'm feeling the energy of souls who used to live here?* I walked beyond that property and the feeling diminished. After that, I would make it a point to walk there and stop to just soak in the energy. That was the first time I had sensed energy like that, but it wouldn't be the last.

I remembered one of the lessons in a Castaneda book about sensing energy. I was intrigued when the elder Yaqui Indian Juan Matus instructed Carlos Castenada to pick a place to sit based on his awareness of how the energy in different places felt to him. He was told to walk around and around until he chose a spot based on the energy there. I thought about that a lot and now I was experiencing an awareness of energy myself.

I was learning to embrace whatever was presented. One night I was driving back to Ellijay, headed north on I-515, when the rag top came unhooked and flew back. My utility car was an early '90s model and the soft top was secured just above the windshield with a press-and-seal latch. It was a couple of years old then, and the rigid plastic loosened from wear. When I was driving sixty miles an hour or so, the soft top would detach and let go. It stayed attached in the back, but I had to stop and grab the front lip, pull it forward toward the windshield, and reattach it in the front. I had done this many times.

On this particular night, I pulled over into one of the paved overlooks to fix the top. When I got out of the car, my eyes were drawn to the sky. Because there were no city lights, the stars were brilliant against the black sky. I stood in awe and said out loud, "Thank you, God, for stopping me." If my top hadn't come loose, I would have missed this absolutely breathtaking phenomenon of millions of bright stars against a huge background of dark sky.

I could enjoy this spectacular scene from my cabin deck, too, but I didn't see the immensity of the sky there because of trees and hills. When I stopped on the highway, I was at the top of a hill and above the trees, so I had an unrestricted view of the sky. If you live in Atlanta and don't venture north or west, you don't have any idea of the seemingly infinite number of stars in the night sky. Thank you, God, for getting me off the beaten path.

CHAPTER 6

WHY START A WOMEN'S CIRCLE?

My next goal while I lived in Ellijay was to start a women's circle, but why a women's circle? The motivation to attain more knowledge and the realization that I could learn a lot from others propelled me to create a women's talking circle in my forties. My appetite for learning from others was insatiable. I liked to meet new people and hear about their ideas.

When I was four years old, Mother and Daddy bought me a picture dictionary. I spent hours sitting on the floor in the living room comparing the color pictures of objects to the words that matched. Soon I had mastered the spelling and meanings of all the words in that dictionary. Then I progressed to *McGuffey's Eclectic Primer* by William Holmes McGuffey, one of a series of books originally published in 1836. I read the Dick and Jane series during the day at school and *Black Beauty* by night.

I don't know why I didn't attend kindergarten while living in Dallas, Texas. Maybe kindergarten wasn't offered, or maybe Mother and Daddy decided to wait and start me in school in the first grade. For whatever reason, I do remember that I was the only one in my class who could read. My first-grade teacher quickly figured out that I could read books and she asked me to read for the class. I was proud when I stood in the middle of the reading circle, but I was also surprised that other children in the class couldn't read. My parents were both avid readers, so I was lucky that they encouraged me and provided books starting when I was young.

Even though my first-grade teacher recognized my ability to read and used me as an example to the class, I was not the teacher's pet. Ironically, I also got in trouble in that class. One day, a boy across the row from me dropped his pencil on the floor. When I reached down to get it, I said, "Here's your pencil." No talking in class except when asked was a firm rule that was taught on the first day of class. My penalty for disobedience was to stay after class and write "I will not talk in class" one hundred times on the chalkboard. I had to take a later bus home, which was scary because I had to wait alone in the gym for the next bus. When I tried to get out, the door was so heavy that I had to push really hard to get out. That initial fear that I wouldn't be able to get out stayed embedded in my mind.

We moved to Arlington, Texas, when I was in the second grade. Daddy and Mother had bought a house and Daddy was eager to get us moved in. My school agreed to let me leave the second grade without completing the last two weeks because I was already ahead. In the third grade, my teacher and my parents met to discuss the option of skipping me from the third grade to the fifth grade. Even though the teacher described me as "conscientious" over and over on my report cards and felt that I was bored in class, the decision was made not to take the option. The concern then was that making friends when you are in class with older students might be difficult. The false belief then was that socialization could suffer if you weren't with those your own age. My experience told me that age had little to do with whether you had anything in common with another student. Actually, when I excelled in a subject, it was easier to be friends with students who were at the same level of learning, not the same age.

When I was in the seventh grade at J. I. Carter Junior High in Arlington, Texas, I was placed in accelerated math classes. I was only moved up in math. The rest of the day I still attended classes in other subjects based on my age, not my ability. The decision was made to move students beyond their grade level in math and science after October 4, 1957, when the Russians beat the Americans into space with their launch of the rocket Sputnik I, followed soon after by Sputnik II. The United States government went into panic mode. One of their strategies to forge ahead of the Russians was to prepare more young people in math and science. Accelerated classes became a big deal.

My math class in the seventh grade was featured in the local newspaper as an example of the efforts to maximize potential in math. I still have the newspaper clipping with a photo of our teacher and some of us students. Throughout junior high and high school, I was in math classes with students older than I was. I dated one smart and witty young man in my math class. He was a senior and I was a sophomore in high school. I just remember that he was tall and wore glasses. He also had a great sense of humor. After he opened the door of his car for me before a date, he got in and tried to strap us both in the same seatbelt. We both laughed.

In an effort to overcome the stigma of being smart, I tried out for the cheerleading team in middle school. This was a sure way to fit in with the popular crowd. I was so proud of my outfit, a blue-and-orange-print dress with matching orange socks. Yes, orange socks. For months, I had practiced with neighborhood girls on all kinds of acrobatic maneuvers, hoping to no longer be pigeonholed as an "egghead." On tryout day, I took my turn on the football field while the judges sat on the lower run of the bleachers. I just knew that all the practicing I had done would pay off and that I would be chosen. I wasn't.

That defeat was rough to accept because it cinched my exclusion from the popular group. I was an egghead, and I might as well participate in egghead activities. Thank goodness, in tenth grade, I was chosen to be on the high school newspaper staff, which was definitely my niche. My daddy had been a feature writer for two newspapers in Connecticut before we moved to Texas. I admired my daddy, so I had a natural interest in being a feature writer for my high school newspaper. Along with two other young women, I was assigned to the feature page. Initially, that was a minor defeat to me because I wanted to be the newspaper editor. After we got busy planning and writing feature stories, though, I knew that the feature page was where I belonged.

My curiosity about people and events came in really handy in the brainstorming sessions about who and what to feature on our page of the newspaper. The radio station in Dallas that played the cool music that high school students listened to was a topic of one page. We phoned and made arrangements to sit in the room with the disc jockeys while the program was in progress. That feature article was a huge success. The students loved it. Even though I wasn't popular, I was recognized.

I drove the three of us to the radio station even though I wasn't familiar with driving in the big city of Dallas. I got a good kidding from Nancy and Terry after I pulled into the exit instead of the entrance to the parking lot and had to back out into heavy traffic. Later, they found a cartoon depicting a driver attempting to enter at an exit and pinned it on the wall over our workspace so they could continue to rub it in. We really liked and cared about each other and we had such a good time working on that feature page. We were curious about what would interest the students at Arlington High School, we liked to meet new people and have new experiences, and we were committed to creating a feature page popular with the students.

***

While living in Ellijay, I continued to brainstorm ideas. After I got my therapy practice started, I mentioned my idea of starting a women's group to some of my clients. I also asked the women in my book discussion group if any of them would be interested in a women's group. After getting a lot of positive feedback, I decided to create a women's personal growth group. The talking circle would attract curious women who had a zest for life and learning and enjoyed exchanging ideas. This was not a support group that focused on personal issues. This was an opportunity to enhance our personal and spiritual growth, together.

We started meeting in the waiting room of the Sailor Drive office after Marion and I had finished seeing clients for the day. I knew from personal experience that women were expected to be nurturers, and we often didn't take time for ourselves. The group was a safe haven where the women didn't have to do anything but show up. If they wanted to join the discussion, they could. If they felt like just listening, they could.

In my planning, I started with themes that I knew were important to women. On one of the first handwritten agendas that I created and handed out to the group members, I wrote words in the margin and around the periphery of the page like "transcend," "enlightenment," "meaning," "fun," "passion," "fulfillment," "purpose," "balance," "letting go," and "laughter." I started out with an idea by Wayne Dyer that we were all teachers and learners in life. The emphasis was that the purpose of the group was to share ideas so that *we all* grew as individuals and as a group.

After Marion moved to the big house on the hill, I found a wonderful space to see clients and facilitate the group on the Ellijay square above a gift shop. After walking up a flight of stairs that was between two storefronts, you walked into a large room that would easily accommodate twelve women. There was also a kitchen, and a bathroom. I figured how to make the monthly rent more comfortable for me by sharing the space with the Gilmer County school psychologist. I had heard from a mutual friend that he was looking for part-time office space. I invited him to look at the space and we agreed that he would pay me to use the space two nights a week. I had already gotten the okay from the property owner, who knew the psychologist.

As we chatted, we learned that we had a lot in common. He sincerely cared about the students, even though he was stretched thin as the only psychologist for the Gilmer County school system, just as I sincerely cared about my clients. He wanted to have a small practice to see adults and utilize a cognitive-behavioral approach similar to mine. We also discovered that we shared an interest in Native Americans and we both loved the Southwest. He and his wife, Judy, had lived in Arizona.

Since I was working full time in my own business by then, I used the space during the day and at least two nights, one for evening clients and one for the women's group. The women became invested in our space, which we called "A Place for Women." They began to bring books to put on the bookshelves to share with each other. Now we had a lending library.

We even dreamed of buying or leasing a big space on some land where we could offer all kinds of services, in addition to the spiritual growth group. There could be yoga classes and massage therapy and reiki. The space would include a walking path down to a gazebo, which would offer women a place to get away individually to meditate and to journal. We let our imaginations go as we thought of how we could expand to benefit the women in the larger community. That didn't ever happen. Circumstances intervened and opportunities appeared to go in other directions.

As I saw the unity building in the group, I got the idea of giving the group a name. At one of our meetings, I said, "What do you think about giving our group a name and maybe a logo?" The women immediately started brainstorming names. One of the women, who was artistically talented, said that she would work on the logo. By the next meeting, the women all agreed to call the group "Butterflies," and our resident artist presented a terrific idea for the logo. The new logo said, "Butterflies . . . transforming lives through personal growth." The logo was encased in swirls of curlicues and under the words there were five butterflies in flight.

What an amazing group of women! I was constantly impressed at the directions of their growth. For example, some of the women took a class in remote viewing, including Louise from Apple A Day Health Food Store. The little bit I knew about the subject was from the *Coast to Coast AM* radio show hosted by Art Bell, a controversial broadcaster and author. Some of the topics of conversation on his show were UFOs, the paranormal, and conspiracy theories.

Remote viewing allows you to see long distances or through paper or walls. On the Art Bell show, there was a discussion about the United States government hiring remote viewers to see what enemies were doing inside buildings on the other side of the world. Of course, the government denied this and so it made for good radio. Did they really hire remote viewers?

The women who took the remote viewing class showed us the steps that they were taught to be able to view objects remotely. A picture was placed in an opaque envelope. They learned to see what was in the picture even though it was inside the envelope. There were many different pictures, one of a waterfall, as I recall. One of the women held the envelope and after a time she could feel coolness. And then an image of a waterfall came in her mind.

Needless to say, I was absolutely fascinated by the way she had learned to train her mind to see what was behind a barrier. Using all of her senses to give her information, she could eventually get an image of the remote object. These women were extremely open to all kinds of possibilities for their personal growth. Many were very creative and imaginative and very open-minded. And they were curious about so many subjects!

Another evening, one of the women told us that she was learning to see auras and she wanted to demonstrate her newly learned ability. So, during the next meeting, one by one, we stood in front of the door that was the entrance from the stairs into the office. And, one by one, she described our individual auras. I had read the 1993 novel *The Celestine Prophecy*, by James Redfield, shortly before I moved to Ellijay. In the book, the main character is taught to see auras by concentrating on seeing the energy emitted by tree leaves. In some spiritual beliefs, auras are the energy fields that emanate from the human body.

This was right up my alley because Castaneda was taught to

see energy fields by Juan Matus, as described in the Carlos Castaneda series of books. Also, in 1996, my daughter Heather and I had gone to Marietta Unity Church to see Neale Donald Walsch, author of the trilogy *Conversations with God*, that was published beginning in 1995. He alluded to the body being encased in a field of energy. An example might be that some people think that the soul is in the body. When the physical body dies, the soul is left to transcend the earthly plane. Walsch's idea is that the soul is bigger than the body and the body is inside the soul. Whoa! I know, it's a lot to think about. But, remember, I like to think about all kinds of possibilities.

When I read *The Celestine Prophecy* in 1993, I sat outside and practiced seeing the energy coming out from the leaves of trees. At first, I squinted my eyes a little bit and just stared at the edges of the leaves. Then I got where I could see the energy coming off the leaves without squinting my eyes. Then I graduated to seeing the energy flowing from people. By the time we talked about auras in the group, I could see human auras. Just white in color. I didn't see auras with any other color except white.

I didn't have to make an effort to see people's auras, either. When I looked at someone, I often saw the energy radiating off their body. It made complete sense to me that we all send off energy. After all, we all manufacture energy minute by minute as we process nutrients and we interact with other people.

A week before the women's group meeting, I had gone with a friend to a gathering of people who were eager to learn from a woman who claimed to be able to "read" people. She talked about various aspects of spirituality in the living room of her big home. At the end of the evening, the host said that she wanted to give each of the ten people present a "reading." When she got to me, she said, "You have a bright-white aura." I was not surprised by her perception of my energy fields. I was just validated.

When we talked about and demonstrated auras that night in my office above the Ellijay square, I was thinking how cool it was to be with women who were so open-minded, who were so thirsty for knowledge, who were so curious. They could entertain many different ideas and sort of play with them, try them out.

I exposed the women to the books and ideas of Stuart Wilde, whose audiotape *Intuition* had given me a lot to think about. Richard Bach, the author of *Jonathan Livingston Seagull*, also wrote a book titled *Illusions* (1977), in which he taught that our *real self* is the playful spiritual being inside all of us. He advocated trying out different paths to see what you can learn from them. As he said, you are always free to change your mind. The women took his suggestions to heart and tried out a lot of different ways of looking at the world, ourselves, and each other.

I began the evening gatherings of the women's group with an opening statement to help let the world outside fade away while we focused on ourselves and our spiritual growth. I knew that many of the women still worked full time. Some had families. Many were going through painful life transitions. This was their time for themselves and I wanted to set up an environment that gave them permission to just *be*. I lit a candle when we began to set a tone and to symbolize Light.

One of the openings that I read to them was from the book *Seven Arrows*, written by Hyemeyohsts Storm, originally published in 1972. I paraphrased it, so this was not a direct quote:

> *Come sit with me, and let us light this candle of Peace in Understanding. Let us Touch. Let us, each to the other, be a Gift. Let us Nourish each other, that we may all Grow. Sit here with me, each of you, as you are, in your own Perceiving of Yourself. Let me see through your Eyes. Let us teach each other.*

I brought in themes and quotes to the women's groups from many spiritual books including the book *Notes to Myself* by Hugh Prather. When Hugh Prather couldn't get published after submitting manuscript after manuscript to traditional publishers, he decided to submit his journal. It had no page numbers, just his day-to-day thoughts. I particularly liked his thought that there is a place where you are not alone.

In 1997, *The Four Agreements* by Miguel Ruiz was published. One of the author's four suggestions for spiritual growth is not to take anything personally. I thought about how hard that is and how sure of yourself you have to be to pull it off.

I also shared Deepak Chopra's ideas in his book *The Seven Spiritual Laws of Success* (1994) and the powerful wisdom of Joan Borysenko in her book *The Power of the Mind to Heal* (1993), which had been published shortly before our group began meeting in 1996.

Many spiritual books were published in the short time span from 1993 to 1998. Many of us who were living in the North Georgia Mountains in that time period believed that there was a convergence of spiritual energy during that time. I believed that I was inspired to facilitate the women's spiritual growth group because my energy converged with a larger spiritual energy in search of evolvement. Even though I had never even participated in a spiritual growth group before, much less gathered women together and led a group, my own quest to evolve spiritually led me to read voraciously and study and take notes to share with the other women.

I crossed paths with many others who were on a spiritual journey during my four years in Ellijay from 1994 to 1998. Some friends had a sweat lodge that attracted those of us with Native American beliefs. As we sweated out the old toxins, we welcomed new guidance. There were friends who initiated rafting trips down the rivers to have fun while we soaked up the beauty of Nature. My counselor friends, many from the Licensed Professional Counselors Association, were part of our fringe group who read spiritual books and formed drumming circles and used our dreams for spiritual guidance.

I took the risk to move to Ellijay while facing so many unknowns because there were opportunities to connect with others on spiritual journeys. I'm not sure when I chose Ellijay that I realized that this was part of some plan for my life. I do know that as a result of my move to the mountains, I met so many people who were searching and studying and gathering together in hopes of bringing spiritual energy into their individual lives and into the lives of the bigger community. We were all drawn to the mountains and believed that there was a reason that we were all there. At that time. In that place.

Chapter 7

What Brought Me to This Place?

What influenced me to take the leap to move to Ellijay where I knew no one, had no job, and took the risk that I would run out of money? My risk-taking, independent, nonconformist essence was molded in my early years. First, Daddy encouraged me to take the risk of flying in an airplane and a helicopter. Second, a dog-training judge mentored me to live up to my potential. Third, a wild Finlander pushed me to ride motorcycles by myself. My husband at the time, Mark, who was born in Finland, encouraged me to ride his big motorcycles long before I bought the 250 cc motorcycle that I rode in Ellijay. I practiced riding around and around our property while he watched and encouraged. Thank you, Mark!

When I was three years old, Daddy was the aviation editor for the *Bridgeport Post* newspaper in Connecticut. He wrote many aviation columns featuring his own flying lessons complete with numerous pictures of Daddy with his instructor. In his newspaper articles, he described flying as "exhilarating" and "fun." He wound up the series by completing his own airman's license. Recently, one of my cousins, the eldest daughter of Daddy's younger brother, sent me a photograph of us in 1950 sitting in an airplane. She shared with me that after the picture, I went up flying with Daddy and she was envious.

I was one lucky girl to have a daddy who threw caution to the wind by learning to fly to make a newspaper column more interesting and then took his only child up into the wild blue yonder. Daddy also wrote many newspaper articles about Igor Sikorsky, who designed and flew the Vought-Sikorsky VS-300, the first viable American helicopter. Sikorsky's modified design became the first mass-produced helicopter in 1942. I was three years old when I got to fly in one of his helicopters. Being adventurous and taking risks seemed natural to me from an early age.

After Chance Vought Aircraft moved from Connecticut to Texas, Daddy took the position of assistant public relations manager at the Grand Prairie plant. Chance Vought Aircraft made airplanes for the navy. In 1954, Daddy was promoted to manager of public relations. As he wrote to a good friend, the money at Chance Vought was better than the pay at the *Bridgeport Post*, but his heart was in the newspaper business and the tight-knit community of reporters. He took a risk and moved his family halfway across the country for the possible opportunities that lay ahead.

Another influence on my life was a dog-training judge named Jack Baird. I would meet him shortly after Mother and Daddy and I moved to Arlington, Texas. I became friends with Lariece Stover, who lived across the street. We both liked dogs and horses. She had a Dalmatian dog and I had a German shepherd. I named my dog Laurie's Quest. The word "quest" means to search long and hard for something that is difficult to find or the attempt to achieve something difficult. The word had a special significance to me when I was eight years old. Forty years later, in 1994, at age forty-seven, I began a spiritual quest after moving to Ellijay.

Lariece and I asked our parents if we could take dog-training lessons at the local National Guard Armory. We wanted to train our dogs to be obedient by following commands like "sit," "stay," "heel," "come," and "jump." After it was apparent to my parents that I really liked training my dog and I really liked the people I trained with, Daddy stepped in as president of the Tri-City Obedience Club and Mother took the secretary position. We were all invested in that activity and enjoyed the community of people.

After I gained some expertise as a trainer and Quest was performing well, we started to enter dog obedience contests. Quest and I made a good team and won many blue ribbons and trophies. When I was eleven years old, we traveled to Houston, Texas, where Quest and I scored 198 ½ out of a possible 200 points in the Open A competition. The reward was a wooden trophy in the shape of the state of Texas with a plaque in the middle. The judge was Jack Baird, a sixty-year-old man with a carnation in his lapel, eyeglasses, and a pipe in his mouth. He presented the trophy to me with a handshake and a smile.

In the same year, Quest and I were in the newspaper again when we won a tracking contest. In the tracking event, the dog sniffed a leather glove that a person had rubbed with their hand to give it their scent. I had trained Quest to follow that scent until he retrieved the glove during many very early training sessions. Daddy drove me to the field about ten miles from our house on Saturday mornings and Mother went along for support. The procedure was that a glove with a scent on it was placed in the field before we got there. From the time Quest started sniffing out the track to the time he found the glove, it was about five minutes.

Jack Baird was the judge again when we won that event by finding the glove before any other team. For the newspaper article, Jack Baird told the reporter that he believed that, at age twelve, I was the youngest person in the United States to successfully train a tracking dog. I had many pleasant encounters with Jack Baird when he judged me in dog-obedience competitions. We became friends and he took on the affectionate name "Uncle Jack." I loved to write and so did he, so we sent many letters back and forth to each other over the years.

When I graduated from Arlington High School in 1965, he sent me the following letter in a congratulatory card that read, "May your achievements of the past and success of the present be only a promise of a still happier future. Congratulations! Deepest love, Jack Baird." The letter that was folded inside the card reminisced a bit, and also was full of guidance for the future. Here is the letter:

Laurie Hyatt, PhD

May 24, 1965

Dear Laurie:

Usually I make up my own cards, but when I can find one as surely fitting as is this one, I retire and send it along.

CONGRATULATIONS!!!!!

Time flies—as I can realize with the very tastefully done Commencement card your class chose. One of the prize exhibits in this unique apt. is the photo of you receiving the trophy from me a few years back, and in the corner of the plastic cover is the most recent snapshot you sent to me. You are in the same exhibit with the photo I have of "Ike"; of Frances Murphy, then editor and publisher of the Hartford Times; and of my dearest friend for 35 years who passed away the day after last Thanksgiving.

The graduation will be memorable, but I hope the Good Lord grants you perfect weather for the event to complete a perfect setting.

What's next my dear? Where are you going now that you have "Commensed"? Whatever it is, and whatever you may elect to do, I shall pray and know that you shall have every success. In this day and age, a full education is a MUST, a duty to yourself, your family, and to life itself. Don't make the mistake that I did and fail to complete your education—of course, I did have the excuse of WWI interfering, and then the need of others for my help—but it's a lame answer.

Boys are interesting, but just keep it that way until you get your degree in whatever field you may elect—and then the world is yours, because the degree is an ace in the hole against any emergencies that can arise—believe me, one doesn't know from one day to another what is going to happen. So do get the insurance of the degree and then consider that nebulous thing known as love and marriage. Don't adopt head and heartaches before you have to do so.

You owe much to your parents and you owe to yourself the pleasure of going forward into Life's battle with the armament that education can provide.

May the Good Lord guide and guard you always is the prayer of your "gruff old bear" of a

*Loving
Uncle Jack*

I'll be with you in spirit that evening and in my mind's eye will see you get that diploma as I got mine 50 years ago.

I was fortunate to have Uncle Jack in my life. His love, support, and guidance contributed to my self-reliance, confidence, and ambition.

Thinking about my dog-training experiences brings back fond memories of horseback riding. I have one heartwarming story and one funny story to tell you about my horseback-riding days. The heartwarming story culminated after my neighbor Lariece and I started riding rental horses at Halbert's Riding Academy in Grand Prairie, Texas. Daddy would take us on weekends and wait in the car while we rode away from the barn, around the wooden corral, and out into a big field. One day, Daddy surprised me by showing up at my fourth-grade class. It was apparent that my teacher was not surprised to see him. He took me out of class and told me that he had bought the black-and-white horse, Beauty, that I always rode at Halbert's and he was taking me to Halbert's for my first ride as her owner. I still remember walking down the stairs with Daddy from my class on the second floor. I was so happy I felt like I was flying.

The funny story happened the next Saturday, when Lariece

and I urged Mother and Daddy to ride a horse. Daddy got up in the saddle and rode his horse with us out into the big field. All went well until we got to the far side of the field, and his horse decided to head back to the barn. Daddy was helpless to stop him. The horse was galloping, with Daddy hanging on to the saddle horn. He managed to stay on the horse, but that was his last ride. He decided that riding horses wasn't for him. Mother's ride was even shorter. She put her left foot in the stirrup, pulled herself up into the saddle using the saddle horn, sat there for a split second, and dismounted on the other side. No more riding for her, either.

Soon, we moved Beauty to a pasture closer to home. In jest, Daddy had told me, "I bought you a horse to keep you off the streets and out of trouble." In fact, the responsibility of caring for a horse was a good life lesson. I also had a lot of fun riding in play days and rodeos after Daddy bought me a quarter horse named Majors. I rode in all kinds of events at the play days, like picking up potatoes on the ground with a spike on a stick. Being a barrel racer was my goal for rodeos, and I soon learned that it takes a lot of skill to gauge just when to lean into the barrel without hitting it. I learned a painful lesson that shin guards are mandatory when leaning into the loop to get around the barrels. While practicing one day, I got too close to the barrel, and the barrel whacked my shin. My leg hurt for a week. I wore shin guards after that.

Many mentors and experiences over many years bolstered my self-confidence, awakened my unconventional streak, and propelled me to take risks, and supported my enjoyment of alone time. Even ten years later when I was in college, I would drive out to the pasture and ride Majors alone, often bareback, just for the tranquility and the quiet and the connection to the horse. In college, I found another way to be a free spirit.

CHAPTER 8

FLYING FREE

When I was a sophomore in college, Arlington State College became the University of Texas at Arlington. One of the new opportunities for students was the Longhorn Flying Club. I noticed it when I was browsing club booths and went right over to find out the details. By today's prices, the rates for plane rentals and instructors will sound ridiculous. In 1966, the Longhorn Flying Club offered students discount rates of $7.60 an hour for plane rental and $7.60 an hour for the instructor pilot, and ground school was free.

I knew Daddy would be thrilled that I wanted to get my pilot's license since he had earned his license years before while working for the *Bridgeport Post* newspaper as the aviation feature reporter. The first step was a physical exam, which included a stress test and vision exam. Even though I wore contact lenses, they corrected my eyes to 20/20, so I passed. Next, I participated in ground school and Daddy was allowed to sit in on the classes. He was amazed at how much I had to know to fly a plane. When he flew, there was no ground school, and navigating meant drawing a line on a map between the starting point and the destination. Now we were learning about fuel and weight and even the weather. I remember my fascination with the various kinds of clouds, like cumulus and cirrus. Different clouds are at differing elevations and some are associated with fair weather and some with potential storms.

After I had finished ground school and passed the written exam, it was off to the wild blue yonder. Even during my first flying lesson, my instructor, Keith, who was in his twenties, had me handling the controls. But first there was the checklist to follow, which included what to check on the exterior of the plane before boarding and a chronology of how to proceed. There was also a logbook to make entries of date, time, and destination for every flight.

Taking off safely in a Cessna 150 two-seater airplane required coordination and the judgment to know when the plane was going fast enough down the runway to start the ascent. Turning includes shifting your weight with the plane. Thank goodness it didn't take me long to feel as if I was one with the plane, and the shifting came almost naturally.

After we cruised for a while, I experienced that sense of exhilaration that Daddy described in his newspaper articles. Looking down at the houses and cars and realizing that I was way above them soaring like a bird was exciting and fun. Yes, I definitely wanted to continue taking lessons and get my license. I loved the free feeling of being disconnected from the ground and realizing that I was being propelled through the air by a machine with wings.

Landing was the hardest part of flying a plane because it required depth perception and being able to judge distance. Keith instructed me to adjust the speed to seventy miles an hour, put the flaps down, keep the wings balanced, and pull up on the nose a bit. This sounds simple, but not everyone has good depth perception. One of the other students in the flying club struggled because perceiving how high up he was from the ground did not come naturally.

I was one of only two females in the flying club. Indicative of the time, most of the members were male. The other female suffered from air sickness, so flying was especially difficult for her. We became friends, and I sympathized as she shared her struggles during the flying lessons. She was originally from Germany. That

December, she invited me and Mother and Daddy to a Christmas event featuring German holiday customs. The fresh Scotch pine Christmas tree was adorned with real lit candles instead of electrical lights and covered with cookies instead of ornaments. I was so enamored with the German cookies like lebkuchen and pfeffernüsse that I made them for our family, punching holes in each one to hang on our Christmas tree. After classes for several days in a row, I spent time in the college library studying German culture. Maybe that's one reason I had a minor in German, which didn't really seem to correlate with a major in psychology. I also wanted to be able to read the original works of famous psychologists, like Freud.

It was very unusual for females to fly airplanes in 1967. Even though women had been involved with flying since 1906 when E. Lillian Todd designed and built airplanes, the number of females piloting planes was still far fewer than the number of males. A funny situation brought it home to me that, as a woman, I was an anomaly flying a plane. Keith and I were flying into Dallas Love Field airport when he had me talk on the radio with the control tower. He turned to me and said, "You talk to the control tower. When they hear your voice, they will be amazed that a woman is flying the plane." When I taxied off the runway, Keith asked me to get out of the plane and walk around like I was just stretching and getting some air, to make it clear to the men in the control tower that a female was flying the plane, even though I was a pilot in training at that time. He thought it was so funny. Flying into airports bigger than the Arlington with one north–south runway gave me the experience of communicating on the radio, landing on parallel runways with commercial aircraft, and taxiing behind commercial planes.

Daddy wanted me to be able to handle the plane if it started diving into a spin, even though it was not required for a private pilot's license. Keith gladly added recovering from a spin to my flying skills. After flying to a high altitude and making sure there were no other aircraft nearby, Keith told me to pull the nose of the plane up until it fell and then nose-dived into a spin. Then down we went toward the earth. I absolutely had a blast when we were spinning toward the earth. Then he showed me the maneuvers that would bring the plane out of the spin, so we could accelerate again and level out. After the first day of learning how to manage a spin, Daddy wanted to hear all about my experience.

When Keith saw that I absolutely loved the thrill of a spin, he suggested we have some fun with rolling the plane. He even got the other flight instructor to go up with another adventurous student and come alongside our plane. We flew side by side, with a good distance between, and then rolled our planes. When the plane was upside down and I looked up to see the earth and down to see the sky, I was laughing with elation. Oh, my gosh, was this fun! When we got back on the ground, I was still euphoric.

After I had logged ten hours of flying time, Keith pulled a fast one on me. We had been doing some "touch-and-goes," which meant taking off, circling around, approaching for a landing, touching the wheels on the runway, and taking off again. Keith shocked me when he pointed to a space off the runway and said, "Stop the airplane over there."

When he started getting out, I became alarmed and asked, "Where are you going?"

"I'll be right over there," he replied. "Just do three more touch-and-goes. Time to solo."

I was scared to death thinking of being up in the air by myself. I had no idea that I would solo that day, but Keith did. When I watched him walk away, I noticed that the other flight instructor was waiting so they could watch me together. It was all pre-planned.

Arlington had a small airport, just a north–south runway with a wind sock and no control tower. Bordering the runway was grass. I gave it some gas, taxied to the runway, and took off just fine. I banked to the left and made a circle back to the runway approach. I thought, *I'll impress them and touch down on the numbers*. At the ends of every runway, there are numbers that designate the magnetic heading of the runway. A pilot who could set the plane down on the numbers of the approach end of the runway was thought to be skillful. In other words, I was going to show off. I was so intent on adjusting my speed and coming in smoothly, wings balanced, putting the wheels right on the target, that when I had accomplished my goal, I was so relieved that I relaxed my grip on the controls. That was a huge mistake. When I loosened my hold on the controls, the eastern wind caused the plane to drift sideways onto the grass. I immediately took a firm hold again and gave it gas and took off again on the grass. I was so embarrassed, but I had learned an important lesson. You are not finished flying until you taxi off the runway, get the plane back where you started, and turn off the key.

I went on to do two more touch-and-goes with no problems. During our next flight, Keith began giving me instructions for cross-country flights, which meant flying from our airport to another airport, landing, getting an official to sign my logbook verifying that I landed at that airport, and then flying back to Arlington.

Keith helped me map out my first cross-county to Tyler, Texas, which was about one hundred miles southeast of Arlington. It turned out to be one of my scariest flying experiences. I remember it vividly because an unexpected storm appeared in front of me before I got to Tyler. I didn't expect the looming storm cloud in front of me and I got nervous. I had to decide what to do, either fly through the big cloud or fly around it. I chose to fly around and watch for the checkpoints on my map to get back in line with my route to the airport. Yes, I literally flew with a paper map. An important part of my pilot training was studying the map before I left, making out a flight plan, noticing checkpoints like buildings, fences, and rivers, and navigating accordingly. I managed to fly around the storm, kept my bearings by noting the checkpoints on the map, and landed safely at the Tyler airport. After I shared my frightening experience with the official at the Tyler airport and he signed my logbook, I flew back to Arlington a bit wiser.

I had learned another valuable lesson: You have to be prepared for any situation when flying a plane and be ready to quickly adapt and make changes when unexpected situations arise. I had to be flexible and think quickly to formulate Plan B, if need be. That experience would serve me well when I took my actual flying test to get my license.

The FAA required forty hours of flight time before you qualified to take the actual flying test to get your license, which included up to twenty hours with an instructor, and at least ten hours of solo, and then cross-country experience. When I reached forty hours and Keith knew that I was ready, he made an appointment for me to take the flying test at an airport not too far from Arlington. We discussed the who, where, and when of my final step in getting my "pilot single-engine land" license. I had passed the written test previously, so the flying test was the last step to get my license.

Keith told me where the airport was and we found it on the map. I would have to fly there, land, get out and meet with the official, fly the airplane with the official sitting next to me giving me orders, and then fly back to the Arlington airport.

As I am writing about that day, my hands are shaking and I feel really nervous. It was a grueling experience, far more difficult than I expected. The morning of the test, however, I felt pretty calm. I was sitting at the walnut-and-maple dining table eating a bowl of cereal while Daddy sat in his usual spot at the end of the couch. He was letting his anxiety show, which was unusual for Daddy. I don't remember being that nervous before the test, but reflecting back on it now, my heart is beating fast.

The day was challenging even before the test began. The first obstacle to overcome was the difficulty of just landing at the airport. There was a tall tree at the beginning of the runway, so when I made my approach, I had to fly over the tree, then pull full flaps to descend quickly to land on the runway. That was the first test and the test hadn't even started. When I got the wheels on the runway and I was taxiing to the designated building, I sighed a breath of relief just to have landed safely.

After I stopped the plane and turned off the ignition, I got out and walked into the building to meet the man who was going to decide whether I got my pilot's license that day. He walked forward to introduce himself and, while I was still standing, he asked me a lot of questions about how to fly. I didn't really expect the questions, but many of them were similar to the ones on the written test, so I had no problem with the correct answers. After that hurdle, we walked out to the plane, where he followed me around the perimeter of the plane and listened as I explained each step of the exterior check. I explained to him that I was examining the plane for any potential problems. With that step finished, we got in the plane and off we went for the final portion of the exam.

He asked me about the instruments and then put me through some expected maneuvers to see how well I handled the plane. As we were flying over a field, out of the blue, he pulled the carb heat, which made the engine die. The "simulating an emergency landing" portion of the flying test had begun. In an emergency-landing situation, I knew that I had to be cognizant that the plane must fly into the wind to maintain lift. This was more difficult than landing at my airport, where the direction that the wind sock was blowing told me the direction of the wind. There was no wind sock in the middle of a cow pasture, but a trick that I was taught was to notice which way the cows were facing. Cows usually stand with their rear ends into the wind. I took that into account, set up the plane for the simulated emergency landing, and just before I would actually put it on the ground, the testing pilot turned the engine back on.

Here's where it got nerve-wracking. The testing pilot pulled carb heat *seven times* at various places, and always with no warning. The engine would die and I would have to figure out a strategy for potentially landing safely. I stayed calm and focused, determined to prove that I could land safely, if need be. It wasn't until I told Keith that he had pulled carb heat on me seven times that I realized how excessive that was. Keith said that he was hard on me because I was a female and he was not accustomed to granting a pilot's license to a woman. Maybe I was the first woman that he had evaluated.

The good news was that eventually he told me to go back to the airport and land the plane. Then he instructed me to taxi over to where we started. We got out of the plane and went into the office. He turned to me and shook my hand and said, "Congratulations! You are now a pilot." You know I had a big smile on my face. He filled out the necessary paperwork, which I took back to Keith, and soon got my official pilot's license in the mail. Unlike a driver's license, your pilot's license is good indefinitely unless you make a dangerous mistake while flying. My license stated that the United States of America Department of Transportation–Federal Aviation Administration certifies that Laurie Alison Innes, followed by my description, has been found to be properly qualified to exercise the privilege of private pilot, airplane single-engine land. Date of issue: 10-07-67.

After I got my license, Daddy was no longer paying for an instructor, but he was eager to pay to rent an airplane anytime I wanted to take passengers for a flight. I just called the airport and rented an airplane for a certain date, time, and number of hours. Daddy and I flew a lot together. In the picture in my album of our first flight together, I have my blonde hair pulled back in a ponytail, and I'm wearing a white button-up shirt with a beige cardigan sweater, light blue jeans, and white sneakers with no socks. On the left side of my sweater are pinned the United States Navy wings that Daddy so proudly gave me. I still have the wings today and cherish them fifty-six years later. In that first picture, Daddy, who was very slim, wears a tan button-up shirt, with a multicolored scarf around his neck and stuffed into the front of his shirt. He had on black slacks and shiny black shoes. The Cessna 150 was red with white stripes. The propeller was silver with gold at the tips. Daddy and I wore aviator-style sunglasses in the picture with both of us in the cockpit. I still wear aviator sunglasses today.

Daddy got the idea of flying to Lake Texoma at the border of Texas and Oklahoma, where we had a weekend lake cabin. It was about eighty miles from the Arlington airport. "I want to take some pictures of that old railroad track under the water. I think there are some big bass in the debris around that track," he explained to me. That was a fun trip. Daddy got a lot of photos, which he later used to figure out where we could go in his boat to get "the big one." Daddy had been in the local newspapers several times when he caught really big fish. A lure company gave him a free year's supply of lures when he disclosed that the secret of his fishing success was their lures.

Mother went up with me too. Her enjoyment of flying with me was funny because she was too scared to get a driver's license. Daddy tried to entice her to drive by buying a new convertible and encouraging her to drive it on the beach at Port Aransas, where there were no other cars. She complied and drove the convertible with top down along the beach. And that was the end of that. No more driving. But when it came to flying, she was not afraid. She and I flew over our neighborhood and beyond the outskirts of town and she was relaxed and smiling. But the minute we got back in the car, she was a nervous wreck, hanging on to the door handle and pushing her imaginary brake from the passenger seat. I kidded her so much about that, and she took it all in good stride. Some days, I went up flying by myself and told Mother about what time I would fly over the house. I would tilt my wings and I could see her waving up at me.

The exhilaration of flying was the freedom to get to the desired elevation and look down at the earth, far below. I would take off by myself to various destinations and I thought about how much I loved being up there, soaring along, high above everything. There were no cell phones then and our airport had no control tower, so there was no way to communicate with anyone. It was really quiet, except for the drone of the engine. I like quiet. I like to immerse myself in an experience, to fully be aware of my surroundings, to enjoy the beauty of the blue sky, the puffy white clouds, the blue rivers and the green trees. That's the beauty of flying without radios and phones back then. I was really flying free.

Freedom has been a lifelong goal for me. When I moved to Ellijay, I was seeking the freedom to spend some time alone and sort out what I wanted to do with my life. I knew that I would be okay no matter what situations arose, but I had no idea what would come next. I have always liked quiet time alone with only myself. As a child, I would go to my room and close the door to study. I would take off with my dog for long walks in the woods, and just sit down and enjoy the sounds of nature. In Ellijay, I had the luxury of evenings alone with my thoughts, entertaining ideas, and contemplating the future.

CHAPTER 9

LETTERS FROM DADDY

On a cold winter night in January of 1998, I drove home looking forward to a quiet evening to do some thinking and planning. I had made no plans for the weekend because I knew I needed to decompress and be alone with my thoughts.

When I walked in the door of my log cabin after seeing clients at my office, I started a fire in the brick fireplace to erase the chill in the house. Then I lit the two oil lamps on the fireplace mantle that were filled with red oil, to add light without the stimulation of overhead lighting. I love the glow of oil-lamp light. The only other source of light in the living room was a lamp on the table. The logs burning in the fireplace, the oil lamps glowing, and the natural pine walls all created a warm atmosphere that wrapped around me almost like a tender hug.

My plan for the evening was to spend some time reflecting on how far I had come in my quest to create an authentic life for myself and to begin to figure out my direction for the future. I grabbed a pen and legal pad, put them on the rectangular pine table just to the right of the fireplace, and put on some hot water to make a cup of peppermint tea. When the water was hot enough, I poured it into a dark-blue mug, and set the mug on the table. Now, the stage was set to do some serious contemplating.

I felt good about creating the women's group, which was so dear to my heart and soul. The women were all supporting each other and challenging each other to grow personally and spiritually. They had taken ownership and created a name and logo, Butterflies: Transforming Lives through Personal Growth. We all were in the process of transformation, individually and as a group. But a nagging discontent was entering my mind. I was realizing that I was no longer able to offer the group new ideas and challenges needed to make progress. So, I wrote down that something needed to change for me to continue to be the catalyst that the women in the group deserved. I needed to bring more stimulation into my life.

After Daddy died in 1981, I still felt his presence. I talked out loud to him frequently, asking him what he thought about whatever I was considering at the time. *What do you think, Daddy?* Daddy's influence in my life continued, not just the encouragement to excel, but also his loving support. I hoped that his wisdom would guide me. I needed some encouragement and guidance right at that moment. As I sipped my tea and held the pen, I felt stumped. What to do next?

Then Daddy's letters came in my mind. At that moment in 1998, I still had every one of the 137 letters that he had written to me from 1968 to 1971. He started writing me letters after I left home when I transferred to Pittsburg State College in Pittsburg, Kansas, in January 1968, halfway through my junior year. I finished my BA in psychology in May of 1969 and an MS in psychology in December of 1970. During those years, Daddy wrote 127 of the letters. I received only ten letters after I received my graduate degree and went to work at a residential facility of intellectually and emotionally challenged youth, Parsons State Training Center in Parsons, Kansas. I kept the letters in two plastic shoeboxes with bright-yellow lids.

I've got all evening, I thought to myself. *Why not get out the letters and read some of them.* I got up from the table and walked across the living room floor into the second bedroom to retrieve the letters. I brought the containers into the living room and put them on the table. Although I intended to read just a few letters, once I sat down and started to read, I couldn't stop.

I took each one out of its envelope and smiled as I soaked up each word. Daddy was a very gifted and witty writer. I had forgotten just how meaningful the letters were, but I remembered that Daddy said to me, "Keep my letters, honeybun, because some day you may write about me." These letters were important to him and to me. I decided to skim though them, lingering on the parts that were especially interesting. Next, I started writing excerpts from the letters that seemed to resonate with me as I searched for encouragement and guidance.

The first letter, sent in January of 1968, was sent in an envelope that he had kept from Hotel Bamer in Juarez, Mexico, where Daddy had stayed while procuring information for his latest publication for Vought Aeronautics Division of Chance Vought Aircraft. The advice about maintaining a sense of humor was not surprising. The warning not to trust easily was something I needed to consider, especially when it came to men. I had been attracted to a couple of guys who were not vested in my interests, and right now my interests were coming first.

Monday, 7:45 a.m.

Hi, Honeybun!

No, I'm not back in Mexico City, although that is in my collection of consummations devoutly to be wished. But I did think that the envelope in which this little communique was delivered might brighten your mailman's day by leading him to believe that one of the new coeds in Tammy Hall is linked with Mexican nobility or---better yet---a long line of Mexican bandits.

I trust you had an uncomfortable night on your mini-bed and meager mattress. All you can do is be philosophical about the whole thing: after all, this has given you a rare insight into what Oliver Twist had to put up with.

I know you're going to be an extra-busy gal for a while so I'll wait until you get settled before beginning to parcel out some of the nuggets of knowledge and pearls of wisdom I have acquired---painfully---over the years. For the moment, though, bear in mind my oft-repeated belief that if we ever lose our sense of humor, we're dead and my strong conviction that most of the people one meets as he tippy-toes through life are no-goods in one way or another (the trick is to determine which way and act accordingly). Many years in the past, when I was a small, starry-eyed and snotty-

nosed boy, I believed in my innocence that all people were nice people. I have since discovered that this is not quite the case. There are not very many 100% nice people inhabiting our universe; the bad guys far outnumber the good guys even though many of those in the first category put up a fine front and are very successful in deceiving the unwary. If I were a young lady, I think I would assume that every male I encountered was a Jack the Ripper or a Boston Strangler until I was damn sure otherwise.

Miss you much and I'm still somewhat staggered at having to communicate at long range (it was so much easier to shout "Hey, you!") with my little teeny-weeny daughter suddenly thrust out into the cold, cruel world. Chances are, however, that I will learn to accept what I cannot change.

More soon. Meanwhile---

Love!!!!!!!!!!!
Daddy

The second excerpt stood out to me for two reasons. Daddy's enjoyment of a fireplace resonated with me because the warmth and glow and crackling sounds from my fireplace at that moment were pure pleasure. More important, though, was his reference to the importance of being different. That was validating to this unconventional life that I was leading, especially as a woman on her own.

Monday – 2/5/68 – 12:15 p.m.
Hello, Bunny!

I was delighted to read your letter and pleased that your advisor has been so helpful (many people are if you give them a chance).

…..Frequently, in my newspaper days, cub reporters and writers asked me how you go about getting stories on the front page with your by-line. The answer, of course, is to dare to be different in your writing style.

….Our fireplace still works perfectly; one of these days I'll nominate this masterpiece as the eighth wonder of the world. Thinking about fireplaces made me wonder how primitive man, once he had discovered fire and built blazes in his caves, ever got around to thinking it might be a good idea to make a hole in the wall to tuck the fire away rather than let it clutter up open floor space…

…. I was happy to hear that my merry missives have made their mark on some of the girls at good ole KSC at P. Confidentially, this has been my secret weapon in my female conquests over the years. Most of the other boys had only virility, and frequently stupidity, to offer and I stood out like a beacon as the lad whose vocabulary included not only one-syllable words but two-and-three syllable words as well. Very effective.

…………………………..Love!!!!!!!!!!!!
Daddy

The third excerpt from Daddy's letters that I chose to focus on captured my attention because of his references to getting checked out in the Mooney aircraft. I did quickly adapt to the differences between the Mooney and the Cessna, and I did get checked out in the Cessna 172 that summer. Also, again Daddy mentions that neither he nor I conform to the norm. So true, and just what I needed to hear as I contemplated yet another unconventional change in my life.

Wednesday – 2/14/68 – 12:55 p.m.
Hi, Honeybun!

No, I haven't forgotten my best gal but I have been a busy boy trying to clear the way to get out of town next week and life at the office has been one interruption after another. ....

......I gather you like the Mooney—if so, stick with it by all means; if not, switch back to the Cessna 150. I guess both the high wing and low wing types of private aircraft have their advantages and disadvantages. I remember the first time I saw the Mooney at the Bridgeport airport one day while I was learning to fly. The Mooney was brand new in the field then and this one was a snazzy, bright red two-place job that seemed to be flying even when it was parked on the ramp. Attracted quite a bit of attention and I recall that I had an urge to fly one of these new hotshots some day [sic]. If you elect to stick with the Mooney, you should be in good shape to get checked out in the 172 or 177 when you come home for the summer. (Not that I'm looking quite that far ahead—I'm counting the days till April). How do you like the retractable gear bit?

.....Enjoyed your last missive. Most father and daughter-away-at-college interchanges are, I suspect, as

dull as dishwater (to coin a cliché) and I am happy indeed that you and I do not follow the norm here, as, much to my satisfaction, we do not follow it in many other ways.

More soon. Meanwhile---

Love!
Daddy

The fourth excerpt was important to my thinking since at that moment I was considering making another radical change that would take me to yet another place where I would be exposed to more ideas.

Monday – 3/4/68 – 7:35 a.m.
Hi, Honeybun!

Your Thursday letter was waiting when we got back from the lake yesterday afternoon.

....pleased by your expression of interest in travel. Too many people have no urge to see other places, to observe for themselves, and to provide a real basis for their thinking about lots of things. I think immediately of Hawaii and the effect of visual evidence, on you and on me...

Love!
Daddy

In this fifth excerpt, from a letter that Daddy wrote while working in California, he was again celebrating the wonders of exploring our beautiful and diverse country. That word "explore" would come up later in a card describing my personality as being an "explorer." Yes, I love to explore places, people, and ideas.

Friday – 3/22/68 – 4:40 a.m.
Motel Lodge, Hanford, California
(pop: 20,000 – El: 232 feet)

Dear Laurie Alison – This America is quite a country we live in – how wonderful it would be if all of its citizens could explore it and see some of the wonders it has to offer in amazing abundance. If any young people approach me today and plead "Kindly and wise philosopher, counsel us as to the future," I'm sure I'll respond something like this: "Get the stars out of your eyes—don't, under any circumstances, buy the bit that the smart thing to do after finishing your education is to leap right into the marrying-settling down-raising a family pattern..."

....Well, bunny, how's that for philosophizing at this early hour in the day?...

Love!
Daddy

In this sixth excerpt that I pulled out, Daddy was showcasing his wit and sense of humor as he made clear to me how much I was loved. I really needed to hear how much he cared about me as I faced confusion. *What I do matters. What I want to do matters*, I thought.

Tuesday – April 9 – 7:35 a.m.
Dear Laurie Alison---

Only six weeks to go, praise be. I must have a word with Mummy about putting the roast in the oven...

More soon, bunny. Meanwhile...

Love,
Daddy

In excerpt number seven, Daddy's prophetic words in this letter about there being some writing in my future really grabbed my attention. Yes, I love to write. What writing is in my future?

Sunday – 4/14/68 – 5:45 a.m.
…..Enjoyed your letter of the 8th…particularly your descriptions of what Mother Nature is up to in Pittsburg. You're real good at this sort of thing, hon – I wouldn't be at all surprised if there is some writing in your future….

More soon. Meanwhile—miss you more than ever.

Love!
Daddy

This eighth excerpt got me thinking about my own religious views. Like Daddy, I tended to be skeptical. I asked questions. I sure didn't know all the answers. I hadn't joined a church in Ellijay, preferring to talk directly with the Creator on my long walks on Mother Earth.

Wednesday, April 24, 1968 – 4:35 a.m.
Dear Laurie Alison –

In a word: "perfect!"

Seldom in life does actual experience come even close to meeting expectations when such momentous events as visiting a darling daughter's college for the first time but our visit to KSC and Pittsburg added up to something extra special in the category of rare happenings.

As you know, I am not easily impressed nor do I strew superlatives all over the place without reason, but the whole bit, from beginning to end, was just flat wonderful. And Mommy....was equally impressed. Matter of fact, "perfect" was the word she used last night to describe the visit as we sat in front of the glowing fireplace and rehashed all the nice things that happened to us.

....Tell Jack that if all the Christians were like him in personality and approach I might be converted from my present belief in Ra, the sun god. Seriously, hon, I regret that it has been necessary for me to formulate my own personal form of religion because I can't tolerate mumbo-jumbo and hypocrisy....I keep asking myself, though, where was the church when some of the ills to which we are now heirs were in the developmental stage. And I have yet to have a man of the cloth, of whatever faith, give me an answer I can accept as to why

outrageous sufferings are visited on little children. This really bugs me.

So much for now, sweetie, 'Tis time for the Distinguished Angler to get with it......,

Love,
Dad

In this ninth excerpt, Daddy's words in the following letter, "individualist" and "nonconformist," certainly rang true to me as well as him. I had not been interested in working for a big corporation precisely because I thought I would lose myself. And, like Daddy, I lived for stimulation and challenge. That's where I was at in that moment, desperately wanting more stimulation and challenge.

Sunday – 4/29/68 – 2:07 a.m.
Dear Laurie Alison –

....The Vance Packard tome I finished up last night, by the way, is "The Pyramid Climbers," which depicted in horrifying fashion the concessions an individual must make to conformity if he is to get ahead in a big corporation...

...Then, when I became manager, it didn't take me long to become completely certain that this was not for me – I was still the individualist, the non-conformist [sic], and, particularly, the perfectionist...

...Well, like you, hon, I live for stimulation and challenges.

Love,
Daddy

In the tenth excerpt from Daddy's letters that I chose to reflect on, Daddy referred to a weekend event that I had attended in Rock Springs. As I read his letter, I tried to remember the details of what was presented, but I couldn't. With my interest in psychology, I went to many weekend conferences, but I didn't remember the specifics of this one. I did jump at the chance to take advantage of experiences that put in a space to meet people and learn about their points of view. Now, sitting in this cabin in Ellijay, I realized that I relished experiences that brought me together with people with different points of view. In this time in my life, I still wanted to expand my thinking.

Monday, 11/11/68

Hi, Honeybun!

Thought of you very, very often during the weekend at the lake....We have read and re-read [sic] your communique of November 4...Your weekend at Rock Springs would seem to have been productive---I feel sorry for all the young people who are not motivated to expose themselves to such interchanges of thought and opinion. But, correspondingly, I'm happy that you have such a keen interest in other points of view and that you are involved in so many activities which bring you into contact with so many new people. This is good!

Love!
Dad

In the eleventh letter that I pulled out, Daddy was referring to my flight instructor, Riley, when I was flying the Mooney in Pittsburg, Kansas. On that night flight, when Riley was teaching me how to fly with only instruments, my dorm roommate, Zoe Ann, accompanied us. We landed at an airport with a great cafeteria and enjoyed delicious fruit cocktail cake. Then flew back to Pittsburg. Funny what I remember—Daddy referred to me as fearless, proud that I would tackle a challenge. I have to say that I did experience fear. I just accepted it and did whatever I set my mind on. Daddy certainly influenced me to do just what I am doing at this moment. Setting off into the unknown . . .

Friday, 11/15/68 – 12:10 p.m.

Honeybun!

I was just plain tickled to death to read the fascinating account of your aerial meanderings over Kansas and surrounding states, to get the hot scoop on your 182 rating, and to swell with parental pride over your accomplishment in getting a flying machine from one place to another at night. Wonderful! Tremendous!

Leading the airborne life of Riley sounds like it can be very much fun indeed---I think you can count yourself fortunate to have encountered this interesting gent in the course of your career as a fearless aviator.

Love,
Dad

In this last excerpt, Daddy was referring to a column that I wrote for the Parsons State Hospital and Training Center newsletter, when I was employed there with the title Psychologist I after completing my Master's degree. Daddy seemed sure that I would be a writer. There it was again. I underlined that word. Writer.

June 1, 1971

Hi, Honeybun!

...Thought your picture in the Parsons paper turned out well and I really enjoyed your column in the hospital publication. I still think you might turn out to be a writer one of these days.

Love,
Dad

What started out to be a few hours of reading Daddy's letters ended up filling the whole weekend. I realized that I was reading them again thirty years after he began writing them. Since those college days, I had given birth to three children, been a wife to three men, and worked too many thankless jobs.

I had also gotten my LPC license and my motorcycle license. I had added tent camping to my list of outdoor activities that I really enjoyed. The book discussion group that I started was still going strong. My self-pay, "do it my way" therapy business was gratifying, but not paying the bills. The women's group that I created and facilitated brought me gratification and added much meaning to my life.

Now, I was reading them with so much appreciation for my daddy and gratitude that I had been blessed with parents who truly loved and cared about me. I also realized that I was a lot like my daddy. I was definitely a nonconformist, a free thinker, an independent-minded person. I liked to spend time alone just thinking, just like Daddy did. Like Daddy, I liked to sit outside thinking big thoughts under the stars. I did my outdoor thinking on my deck, sitting in a rocking chair staring out at the mountain range that they called Walnut Mountain. I also liked to spend hours in front of my fireplace in my log cabin, like I did as I was reading and pondering Daddy's letters.

Daddy had mentioned many times that he thought I would be a writer. I planned to give that a lot of thought. He was also proud of my adventurous spirit and my accomplishments. He defined me as a nonconformist and an individualist. I had no doubt that my next adventure would be met with encouragement and interest by my daddy, as he watched over me in spirit.

After reading the letters, I made some decisions. I was feeling a bit complacent after four years living in Ellijay. What I really wanted was to set some new goals and have some new adventures. What would they be? The obvious pursuit would be writing. I loved to write and had been keeping notes and journaling as long as I could remember. I even underlined phrases and made notes in the margins of the fiction books that I read. That's why I gave up getting books at libraries. I bought books so I could write in them. This might be the time to actually write a book.

Daddy had a lot of magazine articles published, but not a book. He wrote a book about the last man on earth and then scrapped it when he learned that it wasn't an original idea. I had thought a lot about writing for magazines, but was just not motivated to do it. Writing a book appealed to me. I got busy on that project right away. What I didn't know at that time was that a new adventure was also in my near future. I would soon be working on Native American land, where I would be exposed to different points of view about spiritual beliefs, our purpose here on Earth, and the importance of harmony and balance.

CHAPTER 10

ONWARD AND UPWARD

The Monday after my marathon letter-reading weekend, I got busy on my first goal, writing a book. After a productive session with a client who was scheduled for noon, I had a window of four hours before my first evening client at 5:30. I extended my usual note-taking and planning time for that client into a note-taking and planning session for my book. *Onward and upward*, I said to myself as I was settling down to put pen to paper and write my first thoughts about the content. Thirty years after Daddy prophetically advised me in his letters that he thought being a writer was in my future, I was finally making his thoughts a reality. Moving from the office chair where I sat when talking with clients to the plaid love seat, where the clients sat, I asked myself, *What will I call the book?* Almost automatically, the title came to me, *Tools for Living: Taking Control of Your Life.*

Over the last few months, as I wrote down my thoughts and what I thought would be helpful to each individual client, I realized that I was writing similar ideas and concepts for every one of them, which shocked me. Whether a woman presented with relationship difficulties or a man was plagued with feelings of hopelessness, I found myself guiding them with cognitive strategies and spiritual inspiration.

Before each client left the office, I would scribble down suggestions for reading and/or actions that I believed would help that person achieve a more optimistic, solution-focused outlook. After writing my ideas down individually after each session, I had an epiphany. *I am writing basically the same suggestions for everyone.* Instead of repeatedly writing strategic pointers for each client, why not write a book for them to read that included all of the suggestions?

In 1992, I had been inspired by the class Theories of Psychotherapy that was one of two classes required to get my LPC license. I took the class at West Georgia College, driving thirty miles to class two nights a week after seeing clients at my Douglasville office and then driving sixty miles home to Woodstock. The curriculum included an overview of the cognitive behavioral therapy strategies of Albert Ellis. Ellis thought that the long-term psychoanalytic approach to helping clients was a waste of time, like Freud's endless sessions delving into a patient's past. I realized that I had already been incorporating a solution-focused approach into my treatment plans.

During the time that I was taking the class, I was lucky enough to participate in a workshop with Ellis. His wit and sense of humor made the class interesting and entertaining. He explained that he set goals, gave specific advice, and gave his clients homework. We laughed as we sang "Whine, Whine, Whine," a song about the futility of self-pity. I liked the idea of giving clients suggestions in the first session that they could utilize right away and see quick changes in how they felt. I read many books by Albert Ellis, but *How to Stubbornly Refuse to Make Yourself Miserable about Anything—Yes, Anything* was my favorite.

Soon, I developed my own checklist of what to cover in sessions. At the core of each person's unhappiness was the proverbial "looking in all the wrong places" to find contentment. What each of them was completely oblivious about was that they held the power to transform their lives immediately. No need to ruminate over the hurts of the past. They could make life-altering changes by applying basic strategies and merely changing how they thought and what they thought about.

I called my strategies "tools" and I made analogies in my book *Tools for Living: Taking Control of Your Life* to garden tools. Avid gardeners know that you need tools like a hoe, rake, shovel, and wheelbarrow for digging holes for seeds and plants, cleaning up the unwanted and unnecessary weeds, aerating the soil, and transporting materials like fertilizer to the garden. Vegetables and flowers thrive when they have sunshine, rain, fertilizer, live in rich soil free of weeds, and are nurtured by someone who eliminates life-threatening insects, grubs, and snails. Successful gardening is a strategy to make sure the plants have what they need to grow.

Whether I was at my Ellijay office or at my cabin, I began thinking about my ideas and letting them gel. I made lots of notes on what I would include in the book. One day, as we walked into the cabin after a long walk, I mentioned to Trey that I had an idea for a book. He seemed interested in the fact that I was starting a book. Later in the afternoon, he said to me, "I'm going to write a book, too, Mom. It's called *The Blue Elixir*." *Maybe I inspired him*, I thought later.

The Ellijay phase of writing *Tools for Living* was the initial thinking and pondering and writing down my thoughts. I kept notes and started to put them in order. I didn't know then that it would take me two years to finish writing the book and that I would meet many fascinating people who would inspire me and literally help to get the book into print. I didn't know that I would continue to work on the book while having my next adventure in Flagstaff, Arizona.

One evening, as I was preparing to leave my therapy office in downtown Ellijay, I heard Van Tilford's footsteps coming up the stairs. Van was the Gilmer County school psychologist who used the office two nights a week. He was a bit early for his first client and I was in a talkative mood, so we sat down and chatted for a few minutes. I shared with him that I was feeling restless and really wanted to experience a new adventure. "I know that I need to have a new experience where I can learn and grow," I said to him. "Actually, I feel like my group members are ahead of me in their personal growth. I'm just not sure what to do next."

Van responded, "Laurie, why don't you come for dinner this weekend? My wife loves to cook and have company and we can brainstorm some ideas."

Feeling relieved, I eagerly said, "That would be great. Thanks. Just let me know when and what I can bring."

That Saturday, I arrived at Van and Judy Tilford's home and was greeted by friendly smiles at the front door. I hadn't met his wife before, but I readily learned that she had a knack for putting guests at ease and she was a great cook. We had a delightful evening talking about many subjects. Then Van brought up our conversation about my future. "I've been thinking about ideas for you. I just got a new APA bulletin and I noticed that the Northern Arizona Behavioral Health Services has posted openings for licensed counselors to work on Native American lands in Arizona. I know that you are interested in Native Americans, like I am. Do you want to take this with you?"

I felt like electricity went through my body. "Oh, yes! I will definitely follow up on this. I would love to learn more about Native American culture. Thanks!" We bantered for a while about his experiences in Arizona and I learned that we shared an interest in Native Americans. I thanked Judy for the wonderful dinner and the hospitality, and left with a copy of the APA bulletin with a big ad seeking counselors.

This was a turning point for me. I went home and read the ad again. I got really excited at the possibility of working on an Native American land. I started to develop a plan. I would go to Arizona for six months, experience the culture of a Native American tribe, and come back and pick up where I left off in Ellijay. But the more I thought about it, the more I thought about selling the cabin and moving closer to my children when I got back.

The next day was Sunday, so I had time to have a leisurely cup of coffee on the deck and think some more about possibilities. *I could sell the cabin, pay off what I owe, and have some money to travel to Arizona and rent a place to live.* A plan was starting to solidify. What pushed me to act rather quickly was my worry about money. My therapy practice was still not bringing in enough money to pay the bills. I had made a huge mistake borrowing money against the cabin. All I did was complicate my situation. Now, I had another bill to pay, the loan.

The stars seemed to align. I was ready for a new challenge and another opportunity to expand my mind, and selling the cabin would free me up to go to Arizona. Months earlier, when I had visited my cousin Don at his home in Las Vegas, he had given me a picture of yellow and gray baby ducks that was hanging on a wall after I exclaimed, "I love this picture!" I loved the photo of six baby ducks following each other in a line because I could relate to it. The duck that was in the front of the line was struggling to get to the top of a street curb. All but one of the ducks were looking forward, patiently following and waiting their turn in line. I related to that one duckling at the end of the line who was looking around like, "There's got to be a better way or a different way to live your life besides following the leader without question."

That rebellious, adventurous duckling who was bucking the system, who didn't buy into the illogical "We've always done it this way" thinking, who wanted to live her life differently, was me. The comparison jumped right out at me when I first saw that picture.

Like the duckling looking around and considering other choices, I was ready to sell the cabin and spend some time somewhere else. I would fill out applications for job positions on Native American lands in Arizona. I could spend about six months in Arizona and then decide what the future holds back here closer to my children in Georgia. I felt my shoulders relax as I made my decision. When I feel tense, my shoulders knot up and my neck gets so tight I can barely turn my head. Having an idea of what I was going to do next helped to relieve some of my anxiety, even though I was facing a big move across the country.

There was a lot of preparation to do. Three months later, I would be on my way to the next adventure.

Chapter 11

Arizona

Three months after making my decision to pursue the possibility of working on a Native American land, I had sold the cabin and transported my furniture to a storage unit. On a sunny day in September of 1998, I loaded my necessities into my car. It was tempting to put the top down and enjoy the wind in my hair, but being practical won out, so I kept the top up. This was before I had a cell phone and GPS, so my map was within reach in the passenger seat. With a cooler full of drinks and a bag of snacks I would drive the 1,800 miles to Phoenix, Arizona. Three days later, I arrived at my ex-husband, Mark's, place north of Phoenix, close to the area called Cave Creek. I would stay there temporarily until I knew more about where I would be working.

Mark, being the unconventional man that he was, lived in a big metal warehouse. Inside the large warehouse were a sofa and two chairs, a bed, a coffee table, and a television, all centered in a rectangular area in the middle of the warehouse. Off to one side was a refrigerator, sink, and a countertop with a crockpot and, past that, was a bathroom. Mark cooked on the grill outside or in the Crock-Pot, so he had no stove or oven.

I stored my few belongings like my clothes and toiletries, plus sheets, blankets, and towels, in a small yellow building to the right of the warehouse. I took my time organizing everything, so that the display not only looked attractive, but would be easy to load up for my next destination. At night, I slept on the sofa in the warehouse. Even though the divorce from Mark was confusing to me, it was not contentious, and we quickly transitioned from husband and wife to very good friends. Mark was there only on the weekends. During the week, he worked building sets for movies and television shows close to Burbank, California, where he kept a small mobile home in a trailer park.

After I had gotten settled, Mark grabbed some beers from his refrigerator and we went across the street, where he introduced me to his neighbor, Donald. We walked through his house and out to the backyard, where he kept ferrets in big cages. I soon learned that Donald worked as an airplane mechanic for a major airline. Having someone living close by was nice because the area felt remote. He was also a nice guy, and I soon considered him a friend.

When I was still in Ellijay, the Hopi Tribe in northeast Arizona had responded to my application by calling and inviting me for an interview. I explained that I was still in Georgia, and I could be in Arizona within a week. A woman with the personnel department asked that I call her when I got to Arizona and we would schedule an interview. When I called on Monday, she asked if I could do an interview for a counseling position with the behavioral health department on the Hopi land on Wednesday. She gave me directions to the building in Second Mesa and told me to ask for Mark Lewis, the director of the department.

After I looked on the map and saw that the distance from my present location north of Phoenix to Second Mesa on the Hopi land was 235 miles, I figured it was almost a four-hour drive. I felt nervous about driving to an interview somewhere so far away when I had never been there before, so I decided to do a dry run. The next morning, I got up early and drove to Second Mesa and located the building where I would be interviewed.

I drove north to Flagstaff, then turned east to Winslow, then turned north and drove a short distance before I saw the sign for the Navajo land. I was amazed at the long distances where I saw no people and no buildings. Then I drove about twenty-five more miles before I got to the Hopi land. I didn't know that many Navajos were ranchers who lived in buildings called hogans or they lived in mobile homes. As I drove, I observed that the residences were spaced far apart. I would drive miles between one home and another. I saw many sheep, which I learned were a big source of revenue for the Navajo.

Later I learned that there was some friction between the Navajo and the Hopis because the Hopi land was completely encapsulated by the much larger Navajo land. There was no way to get to the Hopi land without crossing the Navajo land. Also, the two tribes had very different cultures and lifestyles. The Navajo, as I observed while I drove, lived far apart from each other and the Hopi, I would soon see, were villagers.

When I saw the sign indicating the beginning of the Hopi land, the scenery changed. Soon, I saw mesas with adobe houses made of clay and straw baked into bricks that seemed to be built into the sides and on the tops of the mesas. When I had called for the interview, I had gotten specific directions, so I learned that there were three main mesas on the land, and I was going to have my meeting on the second mesa.

Before I arrived at the behavioral health building, where I would be working if I got the job, I passed the main administration building to my left where the Tribal Council met and where many government offices were located. I kept driving and started my ascent, and then drove up a long road to the top where the building that I was looking for was located. The rather small building stood alone with parking to the left.

I pulled into one of the parking spaces and turned around before driving back down to the road that would take me back through the Hopi land to the Navajo nation to Winslow, then Flagstaff, and southwest to Phoenix. I felt a little concerned with the remoteness of the area where I might be working. The only other Native American land that I had been to was the Cherokee, and it looked completely different from the arid Hopi land. On my drive, I didn't see any real town with stores and places to stay, like I had seen in Cherokee, North Carolina. I was getting a quick lesson about the differences between Native American Indian tribes, how they live, how they earn a living, and their cultural beliefs.

The next day, I was being interviewed at the Hopi Guidance Center. The director of the Hopi Social Services Program led the interview and several other men also asked questions. They were very courteous and somewhat curious about why I would want to work for the Hopi Tribe. After the question-and-answer session, they reached a consensus on hiring me. Mark explained that they noted that my philosophy of life was similar to the views of the Hopis.

I had explained that I believed that all people, plants, animals, rivers, and living things are part of God's creation. "We are all interconnected and we are supposed to take care of one another. Mother Earth nurtures us and it is vital that we take care of the environment for ourselves, our children, and generations to come. There is a cycle of life that can begin, for example, with a seed that we are given by God to plant. We take care of the plants, and then we harvest the vegetables, fruits, and nuts." I told them that I loved to garden and I felt very close to Mother Earth.

"I think the purpose of therapy is not just to help people rid themselves of symptoms, but to help them make constructive decisions for themselves. I have a holistic approach to therapy, which includes mind, body, and spirit," I said. I also got more specific about my cognitive approach of teaching clients to think differently so that they make different choices. I honor the beliefs and practices of the Hopis and am interested in learning more about their spiritual lives and their cultures. My intention was not to change anyone. I just wanted to help clients lead happier, more productive lives within their own philosophical and religious framework.

After the formal interview, the men told me what they were looking for in a mental health counselor and that my open-minded attitude was as important as my credentials in qualifying for the position. They were very candid and said that they thought I would be a good fit to work in their department with the Hopi Tribe. Mark Lewis explained that I would get a phone call with an offer of a salary, health insurance, dental benefits, and their retirement plan. If I accepted, then paperwork would be completed on my first day of employment. There would also be an orientation day in which all the benefits would be explained in detail. He asked, "Where do you plan to live?"

I replied, "I don't know. Are there possibilities on the land?"

He told me that living space for those who worked on the reservation was limited mostly to schoolteachers and medical staff. "About ten or eleven people who work for the Tribe live in Flagstaff and drive to the reservation in the Hopi van," he explained.

We gave cordial goodbyes and I walked back to my car to start the long drive back to Phoenix. The next morning, I got a phone call from a very nice lady with the Hopi Tribe personnel department who told me the salary and went over the benefits and other particulars of the job. When I accepted, she asked me some questions so that she could start completing the necessary paperwork.

"Can you start next week?" she asked.

"Yes, I'll be there," I replied.

She went over what Mark Lewis had mentioned, that many people live in Flagstaff and commute to the reservation on the Hopi van.

"Where do I get on the Hopi van in Flagstaff?" I asked.

"It's parked in a shopping center on Route 66 in the east part of town," she replied. "They leave at 6:15 every morning Monday through Friday. We will take one hundred dollars out of your paycheck each month to ride on the van."

That gave me a few days to figure out where I was going to live. I called motels in Flagstaff, and got a room that I could pay for weekly not far from the shopping center where the Hopi van was parked. Then I bought some work outfits, including a couple of Southwestern-style dresses. I really liked the long-sleeved dresses with full skirts that fell below my knee. I decided on a pair of comfortable boots, too, because I knew that the uneven terrain requires sturdy footwear.

I originally planned to come back to Phoenix from Flagstaff most weekends, since I didn't want to hang around a motel room by myself. It was a two-hour drive from Flagstaff to Cave Creek, so I could leave on Saturday mornings and get back on Sunday nights. I had brought enough cash to get me by for a while, thank goodness, because the bank where I deposited money from the cabin held the money for two weeks and I wouldn't get a first paycheck from the Hopis for a month.

The next day, I left for Flagstaff to get situated in my motel. The clerk behind the counter was very welcoming and gave me lots of helpful information about what was where in Flagstaff. "A grocery store is about a mile that way," she pointed, "and there are restaurants in the main part of Flagstaff just beyond that." I had noticed that there was a restaurant right next door to the motel, which was convenient. I went to check out my room and was pleased that it was clean and had a microwave and small refrigerator. After I got unpacked, I made a quick run to the grocery store for sandwich stuff, soups, snacks, and drinks. It was getting late when I got back, so I thought I would just walk over to the restaurant for dinner. Looking at the menu, I saw beer listed under drinks. "Do you really serve beer?" I asked in amazement. I had never heard of a Denny's serving beer.

"Sure, what would you like?" the waitress responded.

I was amazed but grateful, because it had been a long, trying day and I just wanted to unwind and relax before bed.

Since the Hopi van would leave the shopping center at 6:15 on Monday morning, I planned to head to the shopping center by 5:45, because I was nervous about finding the van in time. I spotted what I thought was the Hopi van and found a parking spot nearby. A Native American man was unlocking the van.

"Is this the Hopi van?" I asked.

"Yes. Will you be riding to the reservation today?"

"Yes, I will. My name is Laurie."

He smiled and told me that his name was Jeremiah and welcomed me on board. "There will probably be a few more riding today. This is my day to drive. We all take turns driving."

"Okay," I said as I climbed up into the van and found a seat.

A Caucasian man with glasses got on board and took a seat across from me. Then a couple of Native American women found seats together. They welcomed me and introduced themselves.

Jeremiah explained, "We'll stop for gasoline first today. So, if you want to jump out and grab a snack in the convenience store, you can."

Soon, we were leaving Flagstaff, driving on I-40 east. When we got close to Winslow, we made a left turn and headed northeast and then north, where we entered the Navajo land. Before we got to the Hopi land, the road turned slightly northwest. I soon learned that I was the only one on the van who worked at the behavioral health building. I stopped at the administration building to fill out paperwork before heading to my workplace.

When I got to the behavioral health counseling building, I introduced myself to the first woman I saw, who directed me to the office of the clinical psychologist who directed the department. The psychologist greeted me warmly and introduced me to the four other therapists, who were all female. Three were Hopi, as was the director, and one was Caucasian. I felt comfortable immediately. I sensed that this experience would include not only assisting clients, but the opportunity to work with intelligent, earnest, and committed fellow therapists.

My office was down the hall and on the right. I had a desk and chair, a computer, paper and pens, and a love seat in my office. Not long after I arrived, Georgia called me into her office to explain how the department worked. I would see clients individually in my office, for the most part. Sometimes, I would drive a staff car and visit clients in their homes or even at their school. Before I would be checked out to drive a Hopi car, I would have to attend a class on the specific Hopi safety rules for driving.

After I got back to my office and was getting familiar with the computer, a young Hopi Indian poked his head in the door and introduced himself as Lloyd Ami His title was secretary for Behavioral Health Support Services. He proved to be efficient and detail-oriented, which made him great at this job. He was also warm and friendly. I would soon learn that he was also a very talented artist.

That afternoon, there was a multidisciplinary meeting, which included sharing information, goals, and strategy ideas for clients. We all were expected to write reports on each of our clients to share with the group. I had worked in many settings that operated like this, including my first job in Parsons, Kansas, after I finished my Master's degree in 1971. In that position, my title was Psychologist I. At Parsons State Hospital and Training Center, the population was intellectually challenged with some patients who were both mentally challenged and emotionally disturbed.

In my present position with the Hopis, the clients were predominantly adults, some adolescents, mostly Hopi, some Navajo. They were all very intelligent and many were extremely creatively and artistically talented. Most were motivated to effect some change in their lives and were gracious in their gratitude for my time and attention.

They came to counseling for various reasons. Some were ordered to counseling by a judge, for example, for a substance abuse issue. Others came voluntarily for a multitude of possible reasons. They might be depressed or anxious or fearful. Some of my clients would be adolescents who had skirmishes with the law because of alcohol abuse or oppositional behavior.

I liked everyone I worked with and I felt comfortable in this new working environment. I was soon introduced to the four substance abuse counselors and the supervisor of that department. They worked in a building across the road from Behavioral

Health. There were four social workers and their clinical social services supervisor. In addition, there were five family child and support staff with their family support service coordinator.

Mark Lewis, who led my initial interview, was the program director. I knew that I would learn a great deal from these people about their social services program and about the Hopi culture and beliefs. I also knew that I had a lot to contribute to the Hopi community. I was passionate about my work and I loved to see people make positive changes. I thought that there might be a bit of a trust hurdle, but that resolved surprisingly quickly. There could have been a challenge because of cultural differences, but I think my open-minded attitude and eagerness to understand their perspective was an easy read.

I really wanted to live on the land, but when I asked my fellow therapists about possible housing, one woman quickly replied, "It will be hard for you to find a place to stay on the land. There are little houses for schoolteachers and for doctors and nurses, but no housing is set aside for social services. I'll put the word out, though. Maybe something will turn up."

One of the therapists, who was also Caucasian, told me that she had found a small house on the land. It was just a bit of luck that someone was moving out at just the same time that she needed a place to stay. Later that day, I got a call from a woman who had a house for rent, but there was no source of heat. I didn't even look at it, because I couldn't figure out how I would arrange heat and I knew the land got really cold in the winter.

My first day working with the Hopi Tribe was a busy one. I had ridden on the Hopi van and met several other people who worked on the land. I had done the mandatory paperwork and was now officially an employee of the Hopi Tribe. After meeting everyone in my department, I realized how well I fit in because everyone seemed to be committed to the clients and serious about their work. I faced the harsh reality that the drive was two hours to the land and another two hours back to Flagstaff.

When I got back to the motel that evening, it was almost 7:30

p.m. I was tired from the two-hour ride to and from work and from a day of meeting people and learning the routine. After dinner, I looked through the newspaper that I bought the day before. I was looking for apartments for rent or even a room for rent. I called on the room for rent, but it was on the west side of town, close to the university. That would be too far to drive every day to catch the Hopi van. I kept my options open, hoping that I would luck into a place to stay on the land.

After my first week of work on the land, I decided to spend the weekend in Phoenix. I set out on Saturday morning on I-17 south. I decided to take 89A so I could drive along the river that goes through Sedona, which is a beautiful drive. I enjoyed the water running over rocks, and saw several signs about campgrounds, but I didn't see any campers, probably because the weather was brisk. Descending into Phoenix, the terrain changed from the red-rock terrain in Sedona to a more arid look, complete with one huge cactus after another.

When I got to Mark's warehouse, it was much warmer than the temperatures in Flagstaff. I changed into a T-shirt and jeans and drank a bottle of water. As I was driving, I thought about how nice it would be to have another motorcycle. I had missed motorcycle riding ever since I sold my motorcycle before selling the cabin. I went to grab a newspaper and some lunch. The classified ads listed a lot of motorcycles for sale for reasonable prices. I circled a few and made a few phone calls.

When I called about a 700 cc motorcycle for sale, a young man answered the phone. We agreed to meet later that afternoon. I saw that Donald was home, so I went over to say, "Hi!" He told me that Mark was back from California and had gone to a local bar for a beer. I rode to the bar and asked Mark if he wanted to go look at the motorcycle with me. He was in a gruff mood from a hard week working on the movie set and just wanted some time to himself. "Ask the neighbor to go with you," he growled.

Since Donald rode a Harley, I thought he might be interested in helping me get a motorcycle. I asked him to take me to see the motorcycle that I had seen advertised. "Sure, I'll ride you down to look at the motorcycle," he smiled. I rode behind him on his motorcycle and it didn't take long to find the young man's residence. He had a garden hose in his hand, and explained that he had just washed the motorcycle so it would look its best. I really felt bad for him, because he didn't want to sell the motorcycle. He explained, "I hate to sell it, but I need the money."

I liked the Yamaha immediately, with its low-ride profile. I didn't want to show too much enthusiasm, though, because I wanted to get the best deal I could. He showed me the paperwork and was able to prove that he had maintained the motorcycle well. He told me how much money he hoped to sell it for and I made him an offer a bit lower. "I have cash money right now," I said.

"Okay, you've got a deal."

Donald got on his motorcycle and I followed on the Yamaha. After we had ridden for a while, I signaled for him to pull over. "I would really like to buy some saddlebags on the way back. Do you know a good place?"

"Sure, follow me."

We went into a motorcycle shop that wasn't far out of the way to Mark's warehouse. I bought some black leather saddlebags and threw them over the motorcycle behind the seat. They were big enough to carry groceries, books, a spare jacket, and lots of other stuff, and they also made the Yamaha look even cooler.

When we got back to Mark's warehouse, I was really pleased with my purchase and anxious to plan a ride. Mark was sitting outside with a beer in his hand. After he saw my motorcycle and my eagerness to ride, he suggested riding to a biker bar the next day. In that area, Sundays were the most popular day of the week to hang out at biker bars for grilled burgers, cold beer, music, and crowds of interesting people. Sometimes, riders went from one outside bar to another in an afternoon. Unfortunately, motorcyclists have gotten a bad rap from movies focused on motorcycle gangs. Most of the motorcycle riders that I have met just enjoy the freedom of riding and the camaraderie of riding with other motorcycle lovers. Many are also generous and like to participate in rides for charity.

In the past, I had ridden on the back of Mark's motorcycle to various outdoor restaurants, participated in poker runs, and donated toys for Christmas charity events. Usually, the Christmas events were led by a guy dressed as Santa Claus and each of us had stuffed animals, dolls, and other toys strapped to our motorcycles to give away. I rode in Christmas events on my Honda 250 when I lived in Ellijay. One time, I rode to Woodstock and met up with the other riders, who all had toys tied to their motorcycles. The owner of the Harley shop, who was dressed as Santa, kidded me, "Laurie, I like you, so I'm going to make an exception and let you ride with us even though you're not on a Harley." I had strapped a huge teddy bear to the back of my seat to be given to a child who otherwise might not have gotten a toy for Christmas.

Participating in Christmas rides with people who donate their time and money to bring smiles and cheers to little children gave me a sense of pride and satisfaction. One time we rode to a Salvation Army truck in a shopping center parking lot. Another time, we rode to an orphanage and gave out toys individually to the children. No matter where we brought the toys, we all knew that someone's Christmas was going to be a little brighter because we gathered for a worthy cause.

So, I looked forward to Sunday and getting to ride with fellow motorcyclists. I got dressed in my leather jacket, jeans, boots, gloves, and helmet and rolled my Yamaha Virago out of the warehouse. Mark was riding his yellow Harley and Donald joined us on his Harley. I was a little nervous riding my new motorcycle, but as soon as we got going, I relaxed. The motorcycle handled nicely and the ride was smooth. Mark led the way, and I rode diagonally slightly behind, with Donald behind me.

We rode to an outdoor biker bar in Cave Creek, north of Phoenix. The place was packed, so I had to maneuver my motorcycle into a parking spot. The restaurant was surrounded by a wooden fence on three sides. The side to my right was where the food and drinks were served. I smelled burgers and hot dogs on the grill and heard music playing in the background. We walked up to the counter and I spoke up, "I'll have a chili beer and a burger, please." I had been introduced to chili beer, which has a chili pepper in the bottle to add a spicy sensation, at another Cave Creek bar. I liked the flavor and I liked eating the pepper when the beer was gone.

There was seating with long wooden tables with benches, so we naturally were sitting next to other people. Soon, we were having animated conversations with men and women from all walks of life. I was surprised when I met a woman who worked for a company that bought "totaled" cars, then repaired and resold them. Mark noted the old Saguaro cactus which had been brought in and leaned up against the fence for interest. "That Saguaro cactus is probably a hundred fifty years old," Mark told me. "They don't grow their first arm until they are seventy-five to a hundred years old. They are so interesting. I wish I could take it home and put it in the yard."

A few hours later, we decided to head out. I had a difficult time getting my motorcycle out from between the others, since more motorcycles had come in since we had arrived. "What are you waiting for?" Mark remarked gruffly, but with a wink.

"Hold on. I've just got to get out of this tight spot."

In a few minutes, I had the motorcycle freed up and maneuvered onto the road. Away we went, experiencing again that free feeling that comes with riding a motorcycle. Cruising in Arizona was particularly fun because most of the roads are level and you can see for miles in any direction. Once I got in sync with Mark and Donald, I felt a smile on my face from the sheer joy of riding.

We got back about four that afternoon, so I had time to get the motorcycle situated in Mark's warehouse, pack the few clothes I had brought for the weekend, and drive the two hours back to Flagstaff and still be back before dark. In that two-hour ride north, I saw desert country full of cacti, then as I gained elevation, there was more green shrubbery and then evergreen trees. The temperature dropped considerably too. A significant change of scenery and temperature in a relatively short drive.

I pulled into the motel parking lot, got out of my car, and walked into my room. I was glad that I had made that grocery store run and gotten bread, lunch meat, cheese, and chips for a quick and easy dinner. I snapped open a soft drink and watched the weather on a Flagstaff TV station. After a hot shower, I practically fell into bed.

In such a short span of time, I had experienced many adventures: beginning a new job, buying a new motorcycle, sharing experiences with people who were kindred spirits. All this in less than two weeks. What would the future hold?

Chapter 12

From Flagstaff to the Hopi Land

By 5:15 the next morning, I was up getting ready for my second week of work on the Hopi land. Since I had met the van five times the week before, I wasn't nervous about getting there on time. I left the motel in my Jeep at six a.m. and arrived five minutes before the 6:15 a.m. departure time. As I stepped up into the Hopi van, I noticed that there were a couple of faces I hadn't seen before. What surprised me was that the same people didn't ride to the land every day. When I asked Jerry about seeing different people different days, he explained to me, "Some people just go to the land two or three days a week."

I had to ride the Hopi van five days a week since I was employed full time. So did Jerry, who was the IT specialist, and who commuted back and forth like I did. Jeremiah, who supervised construction on the land, also rode five days a week. I also learned that I was expected to drive the van at least once a week. Everyone took turns driving and being responsible for filling up the gas tank with the Hopi credit card.

There was a coffee shop called Jitters close to where we parked the van, and, with time to spare, Jerry suggested to me, "Let's go grab a cup of coffee at Jitters. The coffee is good, but it is really strong, so I suggest adding some creamer." A few others waited until we stopped for gasoline at a convenience store, and went in for snacks and drinks. It was interesting getting to chat with Jerry while we waited for our coffee. He had a cell phone that beamed the signal from a satellite, so his phone worked anywhere on the land.

As I walked by Georgia's office that morning, she greeted me, "Good morning, Laurie."

"Good morning, Georgia," I replied.

"Today they are offering the safety class required to drive Hopi cars that I mentioned to you. Since you will be using cars to make home visits, you are required to take a class to learn about the rules. They have a class today at one p.m., so I signed you up. There will be some other new employees there from different departments. Lloyd can take you over to the administration building about 12:45."

"Okay, great. Thanks," I replied.

The first part of the class met out in the parking lot. A young Hopi woman taught the hands-on class to a small group of us who would be responsible for the safety of a Hopi car and any passengers. We were informed that the credit card for gasoline was in the glove compartment and we were to make sure that the gas tank was kept close to full. Then she opened the trunk and showed us where all of the emergency equipment and other items were. There were blankets, bottles of water, even snacks, in case we were stranded with car trouble or bad weather. She got the jack out of the trunk, and demonstrated how to change a tire. Then, we all had to individually demonstrate changing a tire ourselves.

After the outdoors portion of the class was completed, we went inside and were informed about more rules by a male teacher. He made it clear that when we were driving, we were to keep both hands on the steering wheel at "ten o'clock and two o'clock." "If it is really cold, let the engine warm up before you start driving," he added. Also, "Don't drive until you have completely defrosted the windshield." A couple of months later, I pulled into a convenience store for gasoline. Another counselor was with me because we were going to see a client together. When I was about to pull out, believe it or not, that same instructor who taught the rules portion of the class saw me and noticed that my windshield was not completely free of ice. "Whoa. Wait a minute. Stay there until all the ice is off your windshield," he reprimanded. *Oops!*

The next day, a young woman I hadn't seen before with pale skin, blue eyes, and long, straight, light-brown hair got on the Hopi van in Flagstaff. When she noticed a new face, she said to me, "Hi, I'm Lisa. I'm an attorney for the Hopi Tribe."

"Hi, Lisa. My name's Laurie. I'm working as a therapist in Behavioral Health."

"Nice to meet you. How do you like working on the land so far?"

"I really like the people and the work. I just wish I could find a place to stay. I've been in a motel down the road for over a week."

"Well, I live in Timberline Village Apartments really close to here. I just heard that the apartment downstairs from me just became vacant. Why don't you check it out?"

"Thanks. I'll call and go talk to them Saturday. So, you must not have to be on the land every day?"

"That's right. I've been attending meetings out of town lately. Most of the time, I work in an office in Flagstaff, so I just ride into the land two or three days a week."

After a few more days went by and there seemed to be no possibilities for staying on the land, I called Timberline Village Apartments and arranged to meet someone to show me the apartment that Lisa mentioned. I was greeted inside a large, attractive lobby by Justine Horn, the assistant apartment manager. She was very warm and friendly and told me a bit about the apartments and then we walked to the first-floor apartment that was available.

There was carport-style parking on our right with roofs but no walls, and Justine pointed out that having a cover meant I wouldn't have to deal with an icy windshield early in the mornings. We turned to the left and entered the one-bedroom, one-bath apartment. The living room had a fireplace that used fake gas logs; aesthetically nice, but not practical for heat. The kitchen to the left had a refrigerator, stove, and microwave and the kitchen counter had two barstools. A small space next to the kitchen could be used for a small table and chairs. The bedroom was to the right of the hall and the bathroom was to the left. The walls were off-white and the paint seemed fresh. Big windows were on either side of the fireplace, so the space looked light and airy.

"I like it. Hopefully, we can make a deal on rent."

Justine told me what the monthly rent was, which included utilities. We walked back to the office, where I filled out some paperwork, gave her a check for the first month's rent, and got my key. I could move in immediately.

A couple of hours later, I had loaded up what little clothes, toiletries, and food that I had in the motel, and checked out. Luckily, my parking spot at the apartments was close to my apartment door, so I didn't have a long walk from my Jeep. Since I didn't have many belongings or any furniture, it wasn't long before I had put the food put away in the refrigerator and the kitchen cabinets, had hung up my hanging clothes in the bedroom closet, set my suitcase with my remaining clothes on the bedroom floor, and put my toiletries in the bathroom. I didn't have a couch or a table and chairs or a television or even a bed. Yet.

I decided to buy a futon so that it could double as a bed and a sofa. I called Lisa and asked her for a suggestion on where to buy a futon. With directions in hand, I headed to a furniture store close to downtown Flagstaff. I was greeted as I walked in with a friendly smile, accompanied by, "Hi! How can I help you today?"

"I'm looking for a futon," I responded.

Before I knew it, the salesperson was showing me many styles of futons, more than I imagined existed. I chose a simple, inexpensive futon with no arm support. It was in a rather small box, so it fit in my car easily. One more stop at the grocery store to buy a coffee pot, coffee, food, paper goods, and cleaning supplies, then back to the apartment. I didn't need a coffee cup or cooking utensils. I had brought them with me from Ellijay.

After I put my grocery store items away, I called Lisa, who had offered to help with assembly. She was at my door a little while later, along with her boyfriend, Darrell, a Navajo with long black hair and a warm smile. We got the many futon parts, including lots of wooden slats, spread out in some kind of order, and Darrell took charge of assembly, with Lisa and I as helpers. Darrell left the assembled futon in the sofa position, with the back rest up. I don't know why, but I didn't want it in the bedroom. I guess being back there felt kind of lonely. So, we assembled it and left it next to the kitchen, in the area that could have been a kitchenette for someone with a table and chairs. I was extremely happy with my purchase. The futon was basically a thin mattress with wooden slats supporting it and a mechanism like a lounge chair to raise and lower the back rest. That was the only furniture that I bought in the six months that I stayed there. I was surprised when I slept on the futon that night. It was comfortable.

The next morning, I pulled the back up into the sofa position, and brought a cup over and sat down on my new sofa. *Today would be a good day for a long walk. I think I'll walk to Flagstaff and look around and have lunch.* It was a brisk Sunday in October, a great day for a long walk. I bundled up in layers, a knit top under a plaid flannel shirt and a light jacket. Blue jeans, heavy socks, brown hiking boots, and a knit cap completed my outfit. I headed north and then west toward downtown Flagstaff.

One of the perks of walking is that I notice so much more than I do in a car or even on a motorcycle. Getting to know a new place, especially a breathtakingly beautiful city like Flagstaff, was a fun adventure for me. After I passed the motel where I had stayed, it was mostly new territory, and I soaked it all in.

The most impressive aspect of Flagstaff, Arizona, is that almost anywhere you are in town, you see the majestic San Francisco Peaks. They rise up to twelve thousand feet as a backdrop to the town of Flagstaff, which itself is at seven thousand feet elevation. There was no snow on the peaks that day, but by November, they would stay snowcapped for the rest of my time in Flagstaff.

If I had walked west past downtown Flagstaff, I would have arrived at Northern Arizona University, where I would take computer classes in a few weeks. Lowell Observatory was also at that end of town, famous for the discovery of the planet Pluto. On another weekend, I would visit the observatory, listen to an informative talk, and look at the stars and planets through their telescope. At the east end of town, now behind me, was a small shopping mall and a movie theatre, where I would enjoy the movie *Zorro* the next weekend. I would also buy a buggy full of winter clothes at the huge thrift store.

Now I was strolling into the historic downtown with its many eating places, bars, and independent clothing shops, sporting goods stores, gift shops, and tobacco stores. The tobacco stores carry various kinds of tobacco for Native American healing ceremonies. When I passed the sporting goods store, I had a second thought and went back to buy a compass. I don't naturally have a sense of direction, which means that I'm not good at discovering shortcuts and that I can get lost easily. Because Flagstaff is organized like a rectangular grid, is fairly small, and has many unique shops for checkpoints, I didn't fear getting lost. I was just curious about the directions of my walk.

On the next corner was a truly magical gift shop named Crystal Magic, which quickly became my favorite place just to look around, because everything was so interesting to me. There were, as the name suggests, many crystals in this shop with a metaphysical essence. Many shapes and fragrances of incense captured my attention, so I bought a few sticks to take back to the apartment. I love incense and candles. The greeting cards, many of which referenced numerology, astrological profiles, and personal descriptions, stopped me and lured me in for a long time. I finally bought one that had a big number "5" in the middle of the front page, with "Secrets of Your Day of Birth" at the top and "EXPLORER" at the bottom.

I was born on January 5, which corresponded with the day of birth on the card. But what captured my attention was the word Explorer. I was certainly exploring new horizons in Flagstaff and on Hopi land. I had spontaneously grabbed an opportunity to explore a new land and meet new people. I realized that I was filling my soul by creating a life where the freedom to be myself was paramount.

I am not just comfortable with change. I welcome change. Moving eagerly toward the unknown, which is an Explorer's mission, brings the thrill of uncertainty, of not knowing what comes next. My curiosity is insatiable. Curious about seeing new places and meeting new people, I was exploring new terrain, new ideas, and new ways of life. I was also exploring new career options, like writing and working with Native American people. A sense of discontent had motivated me to travel, which invigorated and energized me. My unique adventure lifted my spirit as I embraced the freedom to be my true self, an Explorer.

In the back nook of the shop, I was delighted to find books. I bought a book on the Hopi people titled *The Book of Hopi* and another very small book on intuition, written by Stuart Wilde. When I finally pulled myself away from the books, I noticed colorful scarves and some long-sleeved blouses. There was also jewelry, including silver earrings with turquoise, and necklaces with many-hued gems. I didn't wear much jewelry, but I did find a simple pair of gold earrings for my pierced ears.

Satisfied to have discovered a space where I felt like I fit in and that I knew I would visit again, I thought about getting some lunch. As I walked back toward my apartment, an Irish Pub was on my left. Just like in Ellijay at the Cornerstone Café, I like to sit at a counter, so I can meet people. I pulled up a barstool, and was handed a menu by a man with a welcoming, "Hello!"

"Do you have any Irish stew today?" I asked.

Gratefully, the answer was, "Sure. I'll bring you a bowl." That simmering, aromatic stew won me over. Now I had found my favorite restaurant, especially when the server informed me, "We have live music on Saturday evenings. Usually a couple of people singing and playing instruments."

"Great! I'll be back soon."

I had a great walk back, taking my time enjoying the reds and purples of the foliage, and looking south and west to large growths of ponderosa pines. The blue sky was clear and the air was crisp. I looked up a side street to my left and spied a small outdoor produce market. A bag of fresh vegetables and fruits hung from my arm for the walk home. I mused about how comfortable I felt in Flagstaff. Many of the buildings were obviously historically preserved and there had been an obvious effort to refrain from high buildings and chain stores. Most of the downtown shops and restaurants and bars seemed to be independently owned and operated, which resonated with me.

In the sporting goods store, I learned that the area was a snow-skiing tourist attraction, as well as a draw for campers and hikers. Lots of outdoor activities brought people to Flagstaff from other states and kept many of the residents busy and active and unwilling to leave. NAU brought many students and professors and the community college appealed to many looking for an employable skill. There was only one drawback to Flagstaff. Real estate was very expensive, so buying a house was prohibitive for many. My apartment suited me just fine.

Back at the apartment, I cleaned and cut up some fresh broccoli, onions, and garlic that I had bought at the market. Then I simmered a chicken breast in a skillet in a little olive oil. I poured some water in a saucepan and added long grain and wild rice when the water began to boil. I heated some water in my coffee-maker and poured the hot water over a chamomile tea bag and left it to steep.

I cooked fresh onions and garlic in a little oil with many meals because the simmering veggies made the place smell so good and made me so hungry. With the meal ready to eat, I sat at the kitchen counter with a plate of food, a cup of tea, and skimmed the book on intuition. "Contented" would aptly describe how I felt at that moment. After cleaning up the kitchen, I relaxed on my futon with some postcards I had purchased at the gift shop. They all had scenic views of Flagstaff. I addressed them to the children, wrote a short note, and added a stamp so they would be ready to mail the next day. There was a small post office on the land within walking distance of the behavioral health building.

My tour of Flagstaff convinced me that this town was my kind of place. I liked the small, independently owned shops, the friendly people, and the emphasis on preserving the environment, especially historically preserving the town itself. The people working in the shops and restaurants seemed to really enjoy talking with customers and adding to their happiness. People who sincerely enjoyed their work, interesting shops with products that I liked, and a gorgeous mountain that had spiritual significance to the Native Americans all confirmed that when I took risks, traveled to places where I had never been, and met new people, I was actually on a journey to find myself.

CHAPTER 13

SACRED HOPI LAND, SPECIAL HOPI PEOPLE

On Monday, I walked to the post office on my lunch hour to mail my cards. This was the first time that I had walked a distance on the land. I like to walk, so I naturally chose walking over driving. I was overwhelmed with an acute awareness of the power and sacredness of this land. An intense feeling consumed me as I walked off the road onto a barely visible dirt road that would take me directly to the post office. There was no one around. No cars were driving on the paved road close by and no one else was walking the dirt path. I was acutely aware of the quiet, and a sense of peacefulness surrounded me. In the silence, I paid more attention to my surroundings. I focused on my footsteps and noticed the aridness of the dirt. I felt as if I were the only person for miles and I could completely experience the spiritual essence of this place that the Hopi Indians called home.

I thought about what I had been reading in *The Book of Hopi* that I had purchased at the Magic Crystal gift shop. According to the author, the Hopis believe that their ancestors migrated over a long distance and turned in four directions before settling in Old Oraibi on the Third Mesa of the Hopi land. Founded before the year 1100 AD, Old Oraibi is the oldest continually occupied community in the United States. The Hopi people had been led by their Creator on a long journey to find their sacred place. At each place where they stopped on their travels, something would happen that would let them know to keep going. They would change direction and go until they felt it was time to stop and, again, they would be urged to change directions and keep walking. By the time they arrived on the land that was their present home, they had changed directions four times. They knew that this was where they were destined to settle. This was land where they were meant to establish villages, raise families, and grow crops such as blue corn, squash, and beans. This was sacred land.

After the Hopis arrived at Old Oraibi, some tensions caused many to keep traveling, so that they settled in twelve villages on three mesas in an area that was originally bigger than the 1,542,306 acres that they currently occupied. The government took away some of their land years after they originally settled, attempting to settle conflicts, including some disagreements with the Navajo, who arrived in the area after the Hopis. The result is that the Hopi land is surrounded by the sixteen million acres of the Navajo land.

Even though the land was dry, with less than a foot of rain a year, they found ways to grow vegetables to feed their families. The Hopi people were resourceful, and grew crops close to springs. They adjusted how and when they planted to be in balance with Mother Nature. The Hopi way of living is directed by their spiritual beliefs. Their Creator intended this space to be for them and their purpose was to take care of the land. They ingeniously figured out how to grow vegetables prolifically and efficiently.

I stopped in my tracks as chill bumps covered my arms. I felt the sacred energy physically and spiritually. Just as I had stopped many times as I walked in Ellijay when energy was intense, I also stopped here on Hopi land to feel the energy overwhelm me. *This truly is sacred land*, I realized, and I was fortunate to be there. After letting myself soak in the experience for several minutes, I finally moved forward, still feeling grateful. I walked the rest of the way to the post office and mailed my postcards.

As I headed back to the behavioral health office, I thought of my experiences with the Hopi people. Last week, I had leaned in the office door of one of my fellow therapists to ask a question about a client. She turned to talk with me and I was drawn to a sign over her desk that read, "How did you make a difference today?" I thought of how conscious she was of her purpose, to make a positive difference. This young Hopi woman and the other therapists felt accountable to others, were serious about their work, and were committed to their clients.

I had gotten another glimpse into the character of the Hopi people one day last week. Just when I was starting to think about lunch, I was informed that we had a visitor in the front lobby. A Hopi woman had walked from her home to sell us some freshly made burritos. I walked out of my office, eager to meet this woman and hoping to buy my lunch.

"How much?" I asked.

"One dollar," she replied humbly and matter-of-factly.

I was absolutely amazed at the work of art that she called a burrito. She had crafted a corn husk into what looked like a little girl with a skirt and a belt and a featureless face. I could smell the steaming meat and onions and peppers inside the corn husk.

"Oh, my gosh! I'll take two!"

After paying her what I felt was not enough money and thanking her profusely, I went back to my office to enjoy the delicious homemade lunch. The food was delicious, but what I vividly remember was the adorable corn-husk doll that encased it. What may have seemed ordinary to the Hopis seemed extraordinary to me. This woman was not only a good cook. She was an artist, creating a meal that tasted good and looked so appealing.

An exchange of opinions at the team meeting that morning also came into my mind. There was some disagreement about treatment for one of the adult male clients who had a substance abuse problem. He was not a client that I saw individually, but the team members explained his situation. He had exhibited some threatening behaviors that some felt required immediate intervention, while one person disagreed. After a short discussion in which everyone had a chance to give their point of view, the director made the decision about a course of action. I respected Georgia, the director, for her knowledge and her calm, yet commanding, demeanor. Without making anyone feel unimportant and after considering what was said, she made the decision for the specific approach that would be taken. I realized in that moment that it was very important to me to respect the people I worked for and to respect my coworkers. I had the utmost respect for my Hopi team of counselors. They were truly special.

I had gotten lost in my thoughts as I walked back to the behavioral health building, so the walk back went quickly. Before I knew it, I was back in my office, greeting a new client. A Hopi man in his forties shook my hand and smiled. After introducing myself and exchanging a few pleasantries, we got to work.

"What brings you here?" I asked.

He explained that he was struggling with lingering feelings of depression. To help me get to know him, I asked some questions about his family history. He shared with me some painful experiences from his past. When he was a young boy, missionaries came and took him and many other Hopi children to a boarding school. His long black hair was cut short. He was punished for speaking his native language. Only English was allowed. He was dressed in "white man's clothes." In the school, he was told that his culture and his spiritual beliefs were evil. He was expected to comply and accept their beliefs as his own, even though his parents had taught him the specifics of his religious beliefs basically since he was born. He was not brought outside or even given a name until he was twenty days old, when he was brought outside into the sun and given a name. The sun and his given name were significant and important, he learned from this ritual.

He had been abruptly taken from his home and separated from his parents, from his entire family, from his village. In the Hopi culture, he explained to me, family includes mothers and fathers, aunts and uncles, brothers and sisters, and grandmothers and grandfathers. They all take responsibility for the well-being of the children. They take seriously the saying "It takes a village to raise a child." Uncles, for example, often play significant roles in teaching boys the rituals and ceremonies that are so meaningful in their spiritual life.

Being taken away from his family by strangers who had an entirely different way of looking at the world was horrendously confusing and hurtful to this man. How could they think that something was wrong with the beliefs that he had been taught? What was wrong with his language, with his hair, with this dress, with his way of living? Years after the traumatic events of his childhood, those feelings of helplessness and anger sometimes reared their ugly heads.

I was purposely very direct with him as I said, "It must be difficult to trust anyone who is not Hopi. I hope I can earn your trust." We worked together on a goal of experiencing himself in the present as being in control of his life. I wanted to help him empower himself to move forward with confidence and optimism. My perspective was that his anger was helpful as long as it didn't consume him. After all, his rights had been violated. He had a reason to be angry. What was not helpful was feeling helpless or hopeless in the present moment. He had no control over what happened to him as a child, but he did have control over his life how. He had been treated inhumanely and called a "savage" years before. Now, I hoped to help him feel empowered as an adult. He was a gifted artisan. He had a family that he loved. He was proud to be a Hopi.

I viewed a therapeutic relationship as a two-way street. We can both learn and grow. I was very open to a client's beliefs and wanted to understand each person based on the framework of their perspectives, spiritual beliefs, and cultural practices. As I gained the trust of my clients and my fellow therapists, I asked questions and listened. I learned about the individual client's life and I learned about the Hopi people.

Some of the Hopis left the land, I learned. They moved to cities where they could find employment. They still often came back to participate in ceremonies and rituals. Many stayed on the land so that they could be involved in the preparations for the rituals and ceremonies that reflected what was meaningful in their lives. One of the ceremonies that caused a lot of excitement in our office was a wedding. It seemed that everyone played a role in carrying out the plans. That sense of community rang out loud and clear to me as I witnessed conversations and activities surrounding the wedding. Family was important. Ceremonies and rituals were important, too, I learned.

Later that week, I attended an educational conference in Flagstaff. I purposefully attended a presentation on Native clans. I learned that there were many Hopi clans. Each clan was made up of more than one family. They were individuals whose ancestry could be traced matrilineally to a common ancestor who gave meaning to that clan's history. Clan members often worked together to carry out social and ceremonial duties and responsibilities, like the wedding that I mentioned.

What astonished me during the presentation on clans was a comment by a Hopi woman in the audience. She was elaborating on the depth of importance of the clans. She shared the name of her clan and then she remarked, "I was born for this clan." She went on to make clear that she was not born into that clan. She was born *for that clan*. That was so profound to me.

She believes that her birth was not random. She did not just happen to be born into that clan on the Hopi land and into that matrilinear lineage. Her purpose was predestined. The purpose for this Hopi woman's life was determined before she was born. When she was born, her family taught her about her individual purpose. She had no doubt or confusion about who she was, and her purpose was clear to her.

Later that night, I couldn't stop thinking about the deep meaning of being "born for that clan." What about me? Was I descended from my mother and my mother's ancestors for a particular reason? I knew little about my mother's mother, Clara Meng Chapman. I don't think she ever worked outside the home, living a traditional role of wife and mother. I remembered her rather subdued smile, her long gray hair pulled up into a big curved comb on her head, and her sense of contentment and her gentle smile.

She had two daughters, my Auntie Grace, who was born in 1910, and my mother, Marjorie Virginia Chapman, born in 1914. Grace Chapman finished high school, never married or had children, and I was like a daughter to her. She worked as the office manager in a legal firm with many male attorneys as long as I knew her. I went to visit her office once, and she was so proud to show me where she worked. However, when she retired, she was angry because the young male college graduate who filled her position had a starting salary much higher than her ending salary. She complained to me about how hurtful that was.

She invested money in the stock market. The Christmas when she visited my family in Marietta before she passed away on April 18, 1985, just eleven days after my son, Trey, was born, she told me that she was leaving me money and she wanted me to buy a bigger house, since we needed another bedroom. I did use most of the money to pay a big down payment on a two-story, four-bedroom house. Brady, Laurie Grace and Trey's dad, paid the monthly mortgage payments on the loan.

Like Auntie Grace, I got my driver's license, while my mother did not. That gave me independence that my mother didn't experience. My mother finished two years of college and had to quit because my grandfather lost money in the Great Depression. He would have lost the house if Auntie Grace hadn't taken up the payments. I perceived my Auntie Grace as responsible, loyal, smart, resourceful, and very warm and loving.

My mother was artistically and musically creative. Her drawings were of people that she knew. I know that I am biased, but she was talented. She majored in art in college, but only drew as a hobby. Another hobby was playing the flute. I have memories of her reading the newspaper in the mornings and books in the afternoon or evening. She grew vegetables and flowers. She also had a sixth sense. Once, she told me that a childhood home burned down and she knew it was going to burn before the fire. When I was in college in Kansas, I called to tell her and Daddy that I was in a car wreck, and she told me she knew exactly why I was calling. She knew about the wreck before I called and she knew I hadn't been hurt.

As I thought of myself being born into this line of females, I could see that I carried on some of their qualities, like being responsible, resourceful, and smart. I took opportunities to push the envelope further, attaining more education, taking risks, daring to move on my own to places completely unknown to me. I was an adventurer, which wouldn't have occurred to my grandmother. It may have been a desire for my aunt and my mother, but I don't think so. I think that I evolved from the traditional female always being loyal to the family and sought out challenges and lived on the edge. I had experiences that they could not even imagine.

You could say that I built myself from a foundation of values like work ethic and being responsible for myself. I also was an avid gardener like my mother, and I have a sixth sense. I have had premonitions many times in my life, but usually vague, not detailed. My reflection on that Hopi woman's statement about her purposeful life pushed me to discover that I, too, was born into a matrilinear lineage for a reason. I was influenced by creative, hardworking women. I was encouraged to spread my wings and have experiences that most women, even in my generation, did not have the daring soul or the courage to even imagine.

My daddy fueled my nonconformity and my discontent with traditional female roles. When I was in the seventh grade, Daddy instructed my homeroom teacher, Mr. Jay, that I was not to take classes in homemaking. Instead, his daughter would take as many math classes as the school offered. He encouraged me anytime I chose to get off the beaten path and go new places and meet new people and have thought-provoking conversation.

I think that working on the Hopi land was put in my path to

help me make sense of my life, why I am here and what contributions I am to make as I grow from my roots to be strong and confident, to ponder the meaning of my life, and to take the risks that lead to my personal growth. I think that I was born into my family which provided a foundation of creativity, intuition, determination, and work ethic. My purpose was to use my talents and to inspire others. Hopefully, my journey will inspire my daughters and granddaughters to fly high and go around any obstacles in their paths to whatever they perceive as a successful life. These special people, the Hopis, were teaching me to focus on my purpose, to clarify my spiritual beliefs, and to open my mind to see myself as part of a much bigger picture.

As I began to drive around the land to see clients, I noticed how many porches were piled high with blue corn, a staple in the Hopi diet. When I asked about blue corn, I was told that blue corn was ground and used to make all kinds of delicacies, from blue corn chips to muffins to tortillas. I wondered how the Hopis grew so much corn in this really dry earth. "Our corn plants are not the tall plants that you are probably familiar with," a lady explained to me. "Those tall plants only yield a few ears of corn, but need a lot of water because of their shallow roots. Our blue corn has deep roots and each plant yields more ears of corn."

Hopi males are put through many tests on their journey to being a responsible adult. One of the tests involves growing corn. The males are instructed to start corn plants from seed in a large underground room called a kiva. A kiva is mainly used for spiritual ceremonies and rites. In terms of the male rite of passage involving growing corn, since the kiva is underground, there is not a lot of light and water must be brought to the room by stepping down a wooden ladder. The point is that a male must take responsibility for his corn plants seriously and be responsible enough to tend to them daily, making sure they have enough water. This is a part of teaching the value of hard work and being accountable not just for yourself, but for others in your family and your tribe.

The piles of blue corn are a testament to the creativity,

resourcefulness, determination, and hard work of the Hopi people. The scarcity of rain is seen as a challenge, a hardship that can be managed. I sensed that the Hopi people never doubted that they could survive on this arid ground when they originally arrived here generations ago. That same steadfast pursuit of a goal that brought the Hopis to this place was still being demonstrated all these years later by their offspring.

As a therapist, I was required to drive to many people's homes to meet with those who had no means of transportation to meet me at the office. Some were women who lived alone. Some were adolescents who did not yet have a driver's license and whose mother didn't have a car. The father might have driven their only car to go to work. The experience of meeting with an adolescent and her mother in their homes gave me the opportunity to see the family as they lived their daily lives. I witnessed their communication patterns and I felt the energy in the homes. The closeness of the families, just as in any family, did not prevent occasional conflicts or struggles. I was honored to work with people who wanted to learn and make any changes that would benefit family harmony.

I also had the experience of working with a family in mourning. A young girl's mother and father had died within months of each other, and she was having difficulty coping and concentrating on schoolwork. I was asked to visit with her at school and work on her grief. I drove to an elementary school to meet with the young girl. A school administrator called the girl out of class, introduced us, and led us to a quiet room in the school library, where we would meet each week. The little girl was brokenhearted, attempting to make sense of the death of both of her parents in such a short time. Her words, "My world broke apart," said it all. She was sad, and she wanted someone to help her. After our first meeting, I looked forward to meeting with her each week. I met her aunt and uncle, who had taken her into their home. The fact that they loved their niece and were concerned for her welfare made my job much easier. She had a good support system with her aunt and uncle, with the extended family, and with the school personnel.

As I left the school grounds that first time, I paused to watch children being taught team-building skills as each of them held an edge of a brilliantly colored red, orange, yellow, green, and blue parachute. In unison, they were soon lifting the parachute into the air, learning that it required each of them doing their part to make the parachute catch the wind. Then, together, they lowered it almost to the ground, and then up again. A beautiful sight to see.

I began to walk more to various places on the land during my lunch hour. After the woman delivered homemade food to our office, I asked if there were other opportunities to buy directly from women on the land. Soon, I was walking up the mesa to women's homes to buy their delicious lunch treats.

I was also honored by being invited to an elder woman's adobe-and-stone home for refreshments. This humbling experience grabbed at my heartstrings. I was told that clay and straw were baked in the sun into bricks for the walls of this adobe home. I was grateful to be welcomed by a lovely lady who invited me to join her for a cool drink. Her home was loved and I felt that her home was special because she lived there. She was special. Smart, gracious, and appreciative of my company. The abode was so fortunate to have her energy bring it to life, and I was fortunate to spend time with her.

Another time when I was awestruck by an elder Hopi woman was during an event that encouraged young people to run. In the past, Hopis were famous for being able to run long distances. Over the years, there was a concern that a more sedentary lifestyle was contributing to diabetes and other ailments. The goal of this event was to promote wellness and to encourage young boys and girls to enjoy the sport of running. This proactive attempt to put a positive spin on running to be healthy and fit and to take pride in oneself was attended by a large crowd. Toward the end of the presentation, the attention of the crowd was turned to a lovely ninety-four-year-old Hopi woman who was walking to the front of the crowd. She was honored and respected for her sustenance. She walked without assistance, as if she were much younger. She told the audience that she had loved running in her younger years and she believed that contributed to her living a long, active life. I was spellbound.

I was inspired by the sacred land and by the special Hopi people. I felt the intense energy of the land and I understood how the Hopi people could be led by the Creator to this place to fulfill their destiny. I was humbled by the Hopi people and their grit and determination to make the best of what was given. They know what their purpose is on Planet Earth and they have a larger understanding of how their actions affect each other and the entire planet. Their ancestors migrated to this land searching for the pre-destined land on which they would fulfill their purpose. That was at least nine hundred years ago. The peaceful, creative Hopi people honor their ancestors by continuing their agricultural lives and continuing to create artisan crafts, in addition to expanding to other pursuits. I have heard it said that the Hopi people are so self-sufficient, so focused on their purpose, that they will survive long after the rest of us are gone. I wouldn't be surprised.

CHAPTER 14

HOPI BELIEFS, HOPI RESOURCEFULNESS, HOPI CREATIVITY

I hadn't worked with the Hopi people long before I had the opportunity to work with clients who taught me a lot about the beliefs of the Hopi people. One day, a young woman brought her five-year-old daughter into my office because she was concerned about her daughter's frustrating behavior. As the mother and daughter sat side by side on my office love seat, she explained to me that the little girl had poured paint into her vacuum cleaner. I made a sincere effort to listen carefully and put myself in the mother's shoes as best I could.

"What do you think caused your daughter to do that?" I asked. I want to emphasize that I was not being cynical. I was completely open to whatever explanation the mother gave me.

"I think she is cursed," she replied.

I took a few minutes to think about what she had said before I responded. I really believe that we all are energy sources. Our bodies and our brains are electrical and chemical manufacturers. Our bodies have energy, and I believe that we can transmit energy. I was open to the possibility of a person being cursed. A person can send thoughts to another person and they can receive them. If the little girl was cursed and, therefore, she was acting in a devious manner, then someone cursed her to encourage her to demonstrate destructive behavior. Even in the culture in which I was raised, in which being cursed would not be a cause for a behavior, the question "What influenced her to act this way?" would be a common consideration. Instead of saying she was cursed, someone might say, "This is learned behavior." Somebody had to expose her to destructive behavior because, otherwise, how did she think to do it?

Whether I literally believed in curses was not the issue. The little girl was old enough to know that the paint would harm the vacuum cleaner. When she poured the paint, she knew that her mother would be distressed. My question to myself was "Why?" If someone cursed her, and I was open to that possibility, why did they curse her? If this was learned behavior, who did she learn it from? Typically, when I worked with young children, I would use behavior modification to encourage constructive actions. In other words, I wouldn't concern myself with "Why?" I would focus on what the behavior was and how to change it. In a behavior modification approach, you would reward her when she acted in a constructive manner and ignore her or punish her for inappropriate behavior. Sometimes, I taught parents how to create a behavior chart that would be hung on the refrigerator or a wall. A reward system would be set up. In this case, the little girl would be rewarded for behaviors that were helpful to her mother together with telling her that pouring paint into the vacuum cleaner was harmful, not helpful.

I mentioned to you before that I was hired by the Hopis because my philosophy of life resembled theirs and because I had no agenda to change the beliefs of the Hopi people. I wanted to understand the Hopi culture and I was eager to learn more from them about how they explain life events, positive and negative. When the Hopi woman shared with me her concerns about her little girl pouring paint into the vacuum cleaner, I was aware that my cultural conditioning would lead me to think that the little girl was being mischievous or oppositional. I might be tempted to say that she was defying her mother or showing out or getting back at her or just thought it was funny.

After being presented with this problem, I needed time to let what she said gel, time to think about a helpful approach. I told the mother that I had raised children and I could understand her exasperation. I asked the little girl why she poured the paint and she replied, "I don't know." It was obvious that my usual behavior modification techniques were not sufficient in helping to find a solution. I suggested that the mother focus on positive behaviors and praise her daughter whenever she did something that was helpful to her. I challenged the daughter to see how many ways she could be helpful to her mother that week.

When the mother and daughter returned the next week, the mother blurted out, "I went to see the medicine man." In the Hopi culture, a medicine man has a special power, the gift of healing. The healing can be physical, emotional, or spiritual. The ideal Hopi life is one of balance, in harmony with Mother Earth, with other people, and within yourself. When you don't live in balance and harmony, you might develop symptoms of an illness or have an accident or behave in an unusual way. Balance and harmony are crucial to the Hopi way of life. The Hopi are a peaceful people. They care about taking care of the environment and they care about each other. They believe that negative emotions like hate, jealousy, and envy can literally make you sick. When you follow the Hopi way, you are emotionally balanced. Harmony and balance define their ideal. The medicine man helps the people establish balance and harmony, and a side effect is that unwanted symptoms disappear. I wanted to work in conjunction with the medicine man. With this situation, I felt that it was imperative that I understood Hopi beliefs, and especially the beliefs of the mother. I decided to spend some time getting to know her better and learning about the role of the medicine man as I worked with her and her daughter.

Another situation arose that gave me a more personal

perspective on the power of a curse. I was told that there would be a meeting that brought together the five therapists in my building with the four substance abuse counselors in another building. Our clinical psychologist director and the substance abuse supervisor would also attend. This would be my first time to walk to that building and my first time to meet those counselors. Before we left, I was warned by a fellow Hopi therapist to be careful while I was in the presence of one of the substance abuse counselors because she had the power to put a curse on people.

The meeting was casual, just a get-together to get acquainted. After introductions, we had time to mingle and get to know one another better. I recognized the name of the woman whom I had been told had the power to send a curse. I made it a point to go over and personally introduce myself and start a conversation with her. Since I had been forewarned, I'm not sure that my perception of this woman was accurate, because I may have been looking for signs of her being different or powerful. What I am saying is that when I met this woman, I felt that she had the power to transmit energy to others. Maybe I sensed it because I expected it. I don't know if she had the power to send negative directives to me or anyone else, but I certainly didn't doubt it. Luckily, she seemed to warm up to me after we met, and I liked her too. What if she hadn't liked me? Maybe she could have put a curse on me. I don't know. I do know that I sensed intense energy from her and I didn't doubt that she had the ability to send a curse.

On another day, there was a third situation in which curses were talked about as the root cause of behavior. A Hopi woman came to my office and told me that she was suffering physical symptoms like headaches and lightheadedness and she believed that she had been cursed. She was a potter who had a reputation for creating beautiful pottery. In fact, her artistic ability was the subject of a long article in a well-known magazine. She shared with me that recently she was driving home when she felt ill. This had happened several times in recent weeks. She couldn't determine a medical reason for her new symptoms, so her conclusion was that she had been cursed by someone who was jealous of her.

My first concern was to eliminate a physical reason for her symptoms, so I suggested she see a physician just to be sure. She gladly cooperated, and the findings were negative. The physician found no medical reason for the headaches or lightheadedness. We met a total of three times, and I learned more about her beliefs and her pottery. We concluded that there was no way to know exactly who would curse her, since she was so well known. We discussed possible stress-related headaches and went over some stress-management techniques. I never knew if she was cursed, but, again, I believe it was possible.

After being exposed to three separate situations in which curses were mentioned, I took time to think about it. The substance abuse counselor who had a reputation for curses definitely seemed to me to be a powerful woman. She radiated intense energy. Maybe the little girl and the potter had been cursed. If so, how could I be helpful? The words "a shield" came in my mind. How could you prevent being cursed? Another way of saying this would be to ask yourself, "How can I deflect negative energy? How can I keep someone from affecting me in a negative way, whether the result is negative emotions, a destructive behavior, or feeling physically ill?"

I thought back to one night when I still lived in Ellijay. A woman in the personal growth group that I facilitated brought up the subject of shields. She shared a specific situation in her life in which she felt that someone had sent negative energy her way. The women in the group discussed ways to put up shields to protect us from negative forces. I continued to ponder the bigger picture of energy, of the force of energy, of negative and positive energy. I was very aware that I respected the various ways of perceiving outside influences, including from curses.

On the way home from the reservation the next week, Jeremiah was driving the Hopi van and accidentally hit a dog who ran across the road right in front of him. Jeremiah was a Navajo who was a construction foreman on the land. Realizing that he had hit the dog, he slowed the van and pulled over as quickly as he could. He knew from the impact that the dog was probably dead.

"Do you have any corn pollen?" he asked Lisa, who was sitting next to him in the passenger seat. Lisa was the young Caucasian woman who was an attorney representing the Hopis who lived above me in the apartment complex.

"Yes, I do" she replied solemnly and pulled up the medicine bag around her neck, unlatched the flap, and withdrew some corn pollen.

Jeremiah got out of the van and walked over to the dog. I watched with fascination as he bent over and thanked the spirit of the dog for his service on Mother Earth. He sprinkled the limp body with corn pollen as a blessing and accompanied the sprinkling of corn pollen with a prayer.

This was a ritual that celebrated the sacredness of life. The Hopis and the Navajo people believed that the dog's life was a gift from the Creator and that it was important to take the time to recognize his life as the dog transitioned from physical life. Although I was surprised that he took the time to have a spiritual ceremony for the dog because I had never witnessed anything like this before, I understood and appreciated taking the time in appreciation and recognition of a sacred life. I learned later from Lisa that corn pollen, which is obtained by dusting it off the tassels of the corn plant, is often used in sacred ceremonies. As I mentioned before, corn is integral to Hopi life. Corn is the first food fed to a baby at the beginning of their physical life and is also used at the end of a physical life to send someone to the spirit world. I learned the significance of having a medicine bag, and purchased one soon after. Even though my black medicine bag didn't have corn pollen in it, I did fill it with objects that I considered sacred. I was honoring the Hopi and Navajo spiritual beliefs by having my own medicine bag.

I was developing love for these warm and caring Hopi and Navajo people and I was grateful for the opportunity to be of help to them and to learn from them. I witnessed how their spiritual lives and everyday lives intertwine. I saw how they survive in this arid ground by being resourceful and studying the terrain, the sun, and the moon before planting. I admired how they live very simply, how they appreciate and care for what they have. They live in small homes and lead lives that seemed simple to an outsider, but, I learned, are based on very complex beliefs and values. Hopis are generally villagers and Navajo are ranchers. Hopis live in villages that have a building with a public shower and many use port-a-potties on the edge of the mesas. Each village is its own community within the overarching Hopi Tribe. Their lives are not easy. They believe that being humble and living close to Mother Earth and working hard for your sustenance are important values.

When life is too easy, you might take what you have for granted. You might lose your reliance on the Creator. I knew before I started working on the Hopi land that the Hopis, unlike many tribes, do not have casinos as an income source. The traditional Hopi elders believe that you must work for what you get. Gambling is easy money and is not the natural order of survival. With traditional leaders making the decisions, the Hopis would not make money from gambling casinos. They would continue to be resourceful and pursue many ways to make money to provide for the Hopi people.

Even though I had seen many examples of the ingenuity of the Hopi people, I was surprised to learn that the Hopis have a variety of income sources. They owned the shopping center where the Hopi van was parked. That explained why the Hopi van could be parked there overnight. They made money from coal mining, even though the Environmental Protection Agency was constantly fighting them. Lisa told me that she spent quite a bit of her legal time protecting the Hopi people's right to mine for coal and to heat with coal. The Hopis also owned a cattle ranch. I was surprised by the business minds of the Hopis, which led them to buy a shopping center off the land and to make money from coal mining and ranching.

Many Native American people are known for their creativity, so I was not surprised that the Hopis are gifted artisans. They make beautiful jewelry, including earrings, bracelets, and necklaces from silver and turquoise and stones. There were gift shops on the land where you could buy jewelry directly or order jewelry. I talked with many Hopi artists who had set up tables outside the cultural center one day. Many young men and women were eager to explain the significance of their work and the steps in the process of getting a piece of jewelry from an idea to a finished product. The bracelets, earrings, and necklaces had intricate designs and pictures representing what was important in their culture, I was told.

The Hopi people are also known for their expertise weaving baskets decorated with symbols in various colors. Baskets still serve a practical service, as they have for generations. Some are large and some are small. I was honored when a Hopi woman made a round basket for me that was the shape of a large bowl. A colleague got me aside and explained that hours of work went into the creation of that basket after time was spent planning the design. Basket weaving is an expected art form for many Hopi females because they needed to run a household. Their beauty also has attracted customers from all over the country, who appreciate the skilled detail of each basket.

Hopi creativity is also expressed in exquisite paintings that depict what I call pictographs and designs. Hopi drawings have been traced back hundreds of years to petroglyphs on rock walls with symbols representing what is important to them, including the sun, corn, snakes, rain, Kokopelli, spiders, animals, jars, feathers, people in costumes, and their own symbols for directions, activities, and the four directions, to name a few. Every piece of jewelry and every drawing has significance and meaning. They are crafted one at a time by individual artists who put their heart and soul into their creations.

Kachina dolls are very important to the Hopi people because the kachina spirits are invisible forces of life in their spiritual beliefs. I observed that kachina dolls were also very popular when I visited a gift shop on the land. I was amazed that there were so many kachina dolls of various sizes and with many differing costumes. This was another example of how the Hopi people express their beliefs through their creations. I admired the Hopi pottery in that shop. The Hopi people are known for the expertise necessary to mold the pottery itself and for the symbolic artwork that adorns each item. Many pots were an off-white color with designs in deep orange and black. I really liked the earth colors of the pottery, but resonated most with the meaning behind each marking. In general, artwork that was superficially pretty did not attract me. I really appreciated the creativity that was demonstrated in the beauty of the Hopi jewelry, baskets, pictures, and pottery, but what was important to me was the fact that the creative process was utilized to express their cultural and spiritual beliefs. Hopi beliefs, resourcefulness, and creativity are expressed in each work of art.

I thought about ways that I am creative. I did not have the talent of the Hopi people to draw or paint or carve objects out of wood, and I didn't know how to make jewelry or baskets. But, just as the Hopi creative talent has been passed from one generation to another, my father encouraged me to express my creative talent through writing and my mother taught me how to create gardens. I also learned that I shared many beliefs and values with the Hopis. I knew that I had not yet incorporated many of the Hopi values into my own life, especially being conscious of the moral goodness or blameworthiness of one's own conduct, but I aspired to acquire their wisdom.

Through conversations and observation, I put together my thoughts on what the Hopi people consider to be wisdom. A true Hopi attains wisdom through life experience and attainment of skills. A Hopi faces life challenges humbly with discernment and empathy. A grounding attribute of a Hopi is respect for Mother Earth, living in balance and harmony with Mother Earth, taking care of the land and relying on the land for survival. Other attributes of wisdom include putting the interests of the community and society ahead of personal gain, and taking the initiative to act in a responsible way without having to be asked or told and without expecting remuneration. A true Hopi wants to give of their time, energy, and talents willingly for the welfare of the community and society. A wise Hopi dreams big and works hard to make their dreams come true.

CHAPTER 15

An Author Is Born

On a Saturday morning in November 1998, I walked from my apartment to the Timberline Village lobby, where residents were treated to free coffee. Justine Horn, the assistant manager who rented me the apartment, hosted the coffee klatch every Saturday. The idea was to give the apartment residents an opportunity to get to know each other. Justine poured me a cup of coffee and we chatted a bit until some other residents arrived. I told her that I was going to start the actual writing of my first book, *Tools for Living: Taking Control of Your Life*, and thought I would structure some time on the weekends. The Saturday coffee time was like going to a coffee shop to work.

After she got busy greeting other residents, I got busy on my writing. I had brought a yellow legal pad, pens, and the notes that I had made in Ellijay. I started by organizing my ideas into a list of strategies that I felt would help people lead happier, more satisfying lives. I settled on a list of twelve tools to be included in the book.

I sipped coffee while I wrote the introduction:

> *Have you ever seen Arizona at night? The sky, I mean. The panorama is monstrous and the blue hue of day darkens gradually as the clouds take on an ever-increasing pink and orange. The colors are surreal. Then another show begins.*

The stars come out, and sometimes the full moon is golden yellow in the horizon.

I came to Arizona to work with Native Americans. I'm a mental health counselor by trade—and by passion. I love the work that I do and the people whose lives I am privileged enough to touch. I've worked in this field off and on for twenty years and, in that time, I've made some discoveries. There are some basic concepts that I find myself teaching clients over and over again. No matter what problem the client presents in the first session, these "tools" seem to be helpful. I call them Tools for Living.

Over the next weeks and months, I developed a Saturday-morning routine of walking to the apartment kitchenette to enjoy a mug of coffee and write *Tools for Living* in longhand. One Saturday, no one else showed up except me. Justine and I spent some time getting to know each other before I started writing. She shared some details about her life situation and I shared some of mine. I really liked Justine. She had an interest in being a writer, too, but complained that working a full-time job and raising a family left little time and energy for writing. When she shared her thoughts, I asked if I could quote her in *Tools for Living*. Justine's words that precede chapter 4, titled "What's Draining Your Energy," capture her frustration:

When I make enough money, I'm so tired I can't write.
When I work less, I don't have enough money to pay the bills.

I thought about the insight of the Hopis' teachings on the importance of balance. Especially for women, getting that balance between work and family, between obligations and self, was difficult. I struggled with traveling a long distance away from my children so that I could venture out to discover my authentic self.

Most mothers will tell you that they feel guilty working outside the home, much less doing something for themselves. Many who work a full-time job, which takes them away from their children for eight to ten hours a day, struggle with an angst about the welfare of their children. In our culture, we women are given the message that we are the nurturers and caretakers. What if you need the money that an outside job provides? What if you would like to earn your own money? What if you enjoy the challenges of a job and the company of other adults? What if you are on a mission to grow spiritually, to expand your mind, to travel to faraway places?

I knew that my life was not in balance. I justified my decision to go to Arizona by telling myself that the closest Native American land to where I was living in Georgia was in Cherokee, North Carolina, still a long drive from home. How does a woman who is also a mother raise a family and also be true to her own passions? Most men don't face the dilemma of time split between family and self. Their role, as defined by the culture, is to be a breadwinner. If they do that well, they are home free. They have paid their penance. All's right with the world. My struggle was that I was not only a woman and a mother. I was a maverick, a nonconformist who didn't like to play by the rules, who didn't adhere to the traditional gender roles. I was a free spirit who wanted to fly once in a while to see what's out there.

Justine was really hard on herself. I knew that the plight of women who divided their time between work and home was the constant feeling that you're not doing enough. I also knew that Justine was a great gal who was being far too hard on herself. One day, I looked her in the eyes and suggested that all the "should haves," "could haves," and "would haves" were wreaking havoc with her psyche. I hoped to lighten her up a little by telling her about a pin I had that read, "Stop shoulding on yourself." Rather than beating herself up over what she didn't do, I wanted to applaud her for all that she was doing, working a full-time job and taking care of a family.

As the written pages of the book accumulated, I realized that it was time to hire someone to type what I had written. I know this sounds funny now, but I didn't have a computer, which wasn't that unusual in 1998. I searched through the yellow pages in the phonebook for a typist and found an ad for "Carolyn Deibel, professional typist." I called Carolyn and made an appointment to meet with her and talk about my project. We met at her office, which was in her home in Flagstaff. After we agreed on a price to do the typing, I left her with dozens of handwritten pages, and agreed to meet with her again the next weekend. Carolyn was not only a typist. She was a stylist who had great ideas for when to bold or capitalize for emphasis, how to space for clarity, and what would make the text look best on a book page. She set up a chart for Tool #12, which was a list of people, places, and activities that were energizing and people, places, and activities that were energy building. I wanted a quote before each chapter and pages so the reader could make notes after each chapter.

Before I left her home, I mentioned that I was having problems with my car. The latch that held the soft top had expanded so that it was difficult to reattach it when it came off, like it had in the past.

"Do you know anyone who could fix it?" I asked her.

"My brother has a dealership in town, Deibel Jeep. Why don't you give him a call?"

I decided to just drive by the dealership on the way home. Her brother explained that the soft top would have to be replaced. After five years of being rolled up and down and being exposed to the elements, the cloth was stretched. The cost to replace the soft top shocked me. The plastic windows had also gotten out of shape and were discolored. Before I knew it, I was talking with Carolyn's brother about trading in my car. I ended up selling it to him and leasing another car.

The next week when I drove into Carolyn's driveway, there was the Jeep Wrangler that I had sold. "Hi, Carolyn!" I greeted her. "That's my old Jeep in your driveway." Carolyn told me that her brother decided to keep it for himself. I felt a pang, and realized I missed it. It was a fun, sporty car and I liked driving with the top down. *Oh, well!*

I was grateful to have Justine in my life for inspiration and Carolyn in my life to skillfully type and format my first book. That support was more helpful than they probably realized. I had traveled to Arizona, first to Phoenix and then to Flagstaff, alone. I carried with me the beginnings of my first book in the form of notes written on a legal pad. I had known that I would begin the actual writing of the book in Arizona, but I didn't realize that I would complete so much of the writing of the book in the five months that I lived in Flagstaff. The energy of the Southwest fueled me to work diligently on my ideas, to put them on paper, and to write and rewrite many times. I had incorporated twelve tools into the book.

I added a chapter at the end that I had not initially planned titled, "The Unveiling of the Soul," which came to me through the process of reflecting on the words that I had written. The writing was more than an explanation of some ideas to give others hope, inspiration, and courage. The writing was also a personal catalyst for insight into my own personal journey of self-discovery. I was examining my own beliefs and the influences on my own life. I was soul-searching.

The quote that precedes the Unveiling of the Soul chapter, "For all my life I've been a seeker," is by Heinrich Harrar, author of the book *Seven Years in Tibet*, which was made into a movie starring Brad Pitt. I related to the words of Heinrich Harrar, for I was a seeker too. I was searching to find my true self, to find clarity and truth, and to create a life that reflected Who I Really Am. The chapter "The Unveiling of the Soul" begins like this:

> *My purpose for being on Planet Earth, I believe, is to remember Who I Really Am, to recognize the limitations that I place on myself, and to pass on what I learn to*

others. Planet Earth, as I see it, is a facility for learning that spins on its axis as it flies around the Sun.

We self-limited humans usually perceive the earth to be without movement. Any rational being can tell by his or her sense of sight and feel the earth is not moving. To previous humans, it seemed to be flat. And humans before that envisioned the earth and sun encapsulated in a huge sphere.

How things change . . . or, rather, how our perceptions of what is Truth change, or evolve.

Several pages later, I wrote the following words:

Making a shift in thinking has been described as a paradigm shift by Stephen Covey in the book The 7 Habits of Highly Effective People. *It is called "moving the assemblage point" by the wise elder Yaqui Native, Juan Matus, in the Carlos Castaneda book series. And others have simply termed it as changing your perception or looking at things differently.*

A prerequisite to the unveiling of the soul includes many shifts in thinking. The soul reveals its true self when there is no blame, no judgment, no fault-finding, and no criticism. When unconditional regard and acceptance are present, soul can emerge.

A few pages later, I wrote:

For my soul to be nourished, conversation must be meaningful, intimate, and have depth. Without that, my mind wanders quickly to other pursuits. The world of money and the material have little importance as my spirit is drawn to the outdoors, to creating gardens and going on long walks

> to a nearby creek. Running water speaks to my soul of movement, of life force, and of the ability to keep moving though there be obstacles in one's path. I must know that everything has meaning and purpose, and it adds to life rather than limiting it. Further expression of Who I Am is this little book, a manual really. It is an expression of my desire to pass some of the ideas that I find helpful on to others. So, Tools for Living *is a by-product of the unveiling of my soul.*

I hope that the three excerpts that I shared give you a feeling for the book that I was working on in Ellijay and Flagstaff. They are but a few paragraphs of a ten-page chapter. In the process of writing that chapter, I was learning as I was teaching. I was exploring my own thinking and discovering my own soul. I truly was remembering who I really was. Just as Daddy said in his letters, I am a writer. I thought back to the many times that my ex-husband Mark asked me, "When are you going to write a book?" When he asked that question, I was too stressed from work and long commutes to imagine putting pen to paper and writing an actual book.

My quiet evenings in Ellijay had allowed me the space to begin the process of writing a book. The Saturday coffee klatches in Flagstaff provided the structure of a time set aside to write. I thought back to the first steps of self-discovery in Ellijay when I asked myself, "What do I want to do with my life?" Now I knew that one goal was to write books. I was a writer and had been since my homeroom teacher in seventh grade, Mr. Jay, made a big deal about a bit of prose I wrote titled, "Poor Little Light." I personified a lightbulb and wrote of its plight of being turned off and on at someone else's whim. Mr. Jay asked me to read it to the class as an example of imaginative prose.

Now, I was devoted to finishing *Tools for Living* so that I could help many people use the life tools that I had discovered. When Daddy suffered from depression, I wanted desperately to help him. That's why I majored in psychology. I wasn't able to help Daddy recover from depressive thoughts and feelings. When he died in 1981 after years of struggling with depression, I was devastated. I continued my search for ways to help people overcome life's disappointments, setbacks, and obstacles. Incorporating what I was learning from my life experiences, I was combining my love of writing with my determination to be of help to others, another of my life's goals.

Many more experiences with the Hopi people would fascinate me. Rituals and ceremonies and unexplained phenomena pushed me to dig deeper, to search for what was real and what really mattered. I was on a spiritual quest, and the Hopi people stirred up a longing to know more.

CHAPTER 16

HUMBLED BY THE KIVA CEREMONY

I wanted to learn as much as I could about Hopi culture. I admired and respected the Hopi men and women that I was fortunate to work with and I remained curious about every aspect of their spiritual life. When I learned that there would be a kiva ceremony, I wondered if I would be allowed to be close enough to witness the rituals.

The Hopi people did not trust easily. That made perfect sense to me after the way that they have been treated over the years. The number of acres that they originally claimed as their sacred destiny has been decreased over the years by the United States government. Government agents were sent to the land to oversee the people and their activities. Missionaries forcibly took children away from their families and made them live in boarding schools where their hair was cut, they could not speak their language, and they were punished for adhering to their spiritual beliefs. When the decisions were made by the government about what land would be utilized for reservations, the Hopi land was surrounded by the Navajo land, so that the only access to Hopi land was through Navajo land. Gang members were another threat. There was a concern about gang members getting into the high school and swaying students away from a life of purpose and toward a life of destructive activities. I attended a meeting where the Hopi Guidance Center staff were taught some of the dangers of gang members who were secretly coming onto the land. For example, if a car flashed their headlights at you, we were told to not respond by flashing our headlights because that can make you a target for a gang initiation of killing the occupants. In addition, people who cared only about money were coming onto Hopi land and stealing valuable works of art. At one of our department meetings, we were told about the extent of the problem of thievery. People would steal the Hopi works of art and sell them, with no regard for the hurt they inflicted. The pain for the Hopis was spiritual and financial.

If someone who is not Hopi is fortunate enough to be able to observe a kiva ceremony, it is because they are trusted to be respectful. In the past, people would show up at sacred Hopi ceremonies and act like it was just entertainment. They would drink alcohol or take pictures, generally having no regard for the depth of meaning that the Hopis associate with their rituals. Because of experiences with those who acted like they were going to a party, rather than a sacred ritual, the Hopi were mindful of who they allowed to watch the kiva ceremony. The rules were that there was no alcohol, just as there is no alcohol allowed on the entire land. Also, you could not take pictures or make audio recordings.

I was honored to be invited to the kiva ceremony. A fellow employee told me when and where the kiva ceremony would take place on the land. I was cautioned that I could not enter the underground kiva structure. I could watch the proceedings from ground level as the Hopi men entered the kiva, I could look down into the kiva to see them dance, and I could watch as they left the kiva. The rituals were very important to the Hopis who participated or attended, and, in the Hopi beliefs, the rituals were vital to the existence of the entire world. I was amazed at how tuned in the Hopis were with Mother Earth. They maintained a direct connection with the Creator and with Mother Earth as they planted and reaped their crops and as they danced and chanted to keep the Earth in balance.

The Hopis who participated in that evening's kiva ceremony were keenly aware that the balance of the Earth is precarious. They knew that the Earth is spinning around the sun on its axis at an angle. They believed that what people do directly affects the stability of the Earth. Most important, they felt a great responsibility to keep the Earth balanced on its axis, particularly around the end of the year and beginning of the new year when it is most vulnerable. The Earth's rotation on its own axis while it also rotates in space affects not just the planet, but the entire universe. By dancing and chanting in the kiva, the Hopi men were literally keeping Mother Earth in balance and the other planets in their orbits. The Hopi were concerned with the bigger picture of existence, not just individual human existence.

I so wanted to know more about the Hopi beliefs and I thought that being able to observe a kiva ceremony would help me have a deeper understanding of the importance of their rituals. After another therapist and I arrived at the designated place on the land, we walked toward the kiva and stood as close as we were allowed to stand. The kiva that we were standing above was an underground square building. The men entered and left the kiva on a ladder made of wood. The top of the ladder was a couple of feet higher than the kiva entrance, so you could sometimes see a kiva from a distance because you could see the top of the ladder. When I looked down into the kiva, I noticed that benches were arranged against the walls for seating. We all stood quietly, waiting for the men to arrive.

The men's ceremonial entrance took my breath away. Each man was in costume from the top of his head to the bottom of his feet. Each unique costume was adorned with meaningful markings and symbols. They walked solemnly in single file toward the entrance to the kiva. I couldn't believe that I was really there, really witnessing this fascinating ceremony, really this fortunate to be with a people who take their responsibilities to maintain the balance of Mother Earth so seriously.

As the participants descended the ladder one by one, some sat down on the benches against the walls. Others began to dance and chant. Rhythmically, they put one foot in front of the other, in step with the man in front of them. The dancing and chanting seemed hypnotic. Their movements and their chants were purposeful and originated in the depths of their souls. Completely entranced by the cadence and the sounds of the men dancing in rhythm, I stood spellbound. I was honored to be able to witness these people working to keep the Earth in balance, just as their ancestors had done for hundreds of years. If the Hopis arrived in Oraibi no later than 1100 AD, then they have been repeating this ritual on this land for at least nine hundred years. I imagined that this ritual originated many, many years before their arrival in Arizona, so the Hopi have probably been dedicated to maintaining the Earth's balance for well over a thousand years. The consistency of this ritual being passed on from one generation to another for so many years is a remarkable legacy.

Entranced by the steady beat, time seemed to stand still. I have no idea how long I stood there and how long they danced and chanted, but eventually they began to climb the ladder one by one, solemnly. I was mesmerized by their bright-colored costumes and their somber attitudes, by their deep belief in what they were doing and their obligation to their people, to Mother Earth, and beyond. I studied their somber faces and felt their intense energy as they climbed the kiva ladder one by one. Soon, they had all disappeared and I found it hard to move. I was still in the moment, captivated by what I witnessed.

I was so fortunate to have that experience. I had watched magic happen. I had observed a people who have followed the teachings of their ancestors for generations continue their sacred rituals. The next week, I thought again about how disrespectful it was for people to come onto the land to steal artifacts from the Hopis. Especially after what I had seen at the kiva ceremony, I could not fathom how anyone could steal their pottery, jewelry, and paintings for the sole purpose of making money. I could not fathom how anyone could disrespect these wise, honest, and hardworking people. How could they come onto the land only to steal the Hopi sacred objects and sell them as a means to make money? I could not comprehend this soulless behavior. I knew that people who were peaceful were often taken advantage of by people who lived superficially from one day to another solely focusing on themselves and not caring about the feelings of others. When I saw such extraordinary people being victimized, I felt angry.

I learned so much from the Hopi people as they demonstrated their firm values and clear beliefs. They took care of the earth and they took care of each other. They worked to maintain balance in their own lives and balance in the environment. Even though their people had a firm foundation of values and purpose, as demonstrated by the kiva ceremony, some had difficulty maintaining balance in their personal lives. Some had lost themselves in alcohol. Some had difficulty maintaining healthy relationships. Some had lost touch with the depth of purpose in the ancient rituals. Some had made choices to live off the land to find work because the opportunities for employment on the land were limited. Many struggled in poverty. Individually, the Hopis experienced challenges and tragedies and difficulties. Some had lost their way. I had a window into some of their lives as I worked with many of them in therapy.

Northland Pioneer College, a community college founded in 1974, was accessible to those who wished to increase the chances of attaining a skill that would translate to a job that would adequately provide for their families. Many worked in construction on the land. Some taught school. Some worked in the medical field in the hospital and other medical facilities. Some operated small grocery stores with gas stations or restaurants or gift shops. Many sold their beautiful crafts. They strived to maintain the balance and harmony that were so important to the Hopi people. When I worked on the land, I was respected and, yes, I would say I was loved, just as I respected and loved the Hopis.

My nonconformist free spirit took me to Arizona to work with the Hopis. They taught me so much. I discovered so much about myself. From the kiva ceremony and from the Hopi people who touched my spirit, I became aware of the importance of balance. I found kindred spirits all the way across the United States. Like the Hopis, I felt a sacred connection to Mother Earth. I believed that I had a responsibility to take care of Mother Earth and to show my appreciation for the many gifts that she offers. We all have a responsibility to care for her just as she nurtures us. I learned the importance of being authentic in my beliefs and my actions. I learned that the spiritual life of the Hopis is rich with beauty, meaning, and purpose. The traditional Hopis put the Creator and their spiritual life ahead of all else. Though I sometimes faltered in my efforts, I sought to remember who I was, a gift from the Creator. My life was a gift and I had a responsibility to appreciate how fortunate I was to wake up each morning on this beautiful planet that still spins on its axis through space, with billions of us humans on board.

My awareness of the precariousness of the Earth's tilted axis was increased by the wisdom of a people who have continued the teachings of their ancestors. They continue to hold rituals and ceremonies to keep the Earth in balance. Like their forefathers, the Hopis have for many generations worked the soil under the most difficult conditions and managed to feed their families. They believe that long after many other cultures who are not connected to Mother Earth are only found in history books, the Hopi people will have survived. They believe that they will survive because they have followed the dictates of their ancestors. They survive because they continue to balance their lives by putting their relationship with the Creator and with Mother Earth foremost in their minds and in their actions.

Like the Hopis, who have refused to conform to the values of the dominant society, I was also a nonconformist. Just as the Hopis refused to make a fast buck, I have not concerned myself with what other people are doing, how much they have, as so many who follow the Western culture mandate of "He who has the most stuff wins." The balanced way of living simply with my feet firmly planted on the ground parallels the values of the Hopi people. They work hard to exist. What brought me to my knees was the deep belief of the Hopi people that when they follow the ancient teachings, observe the sun and the moon and seek out springs of water to grow their crops, follow the cycles of Nature, continue to seek a balanced life, they will live in harmony with the Creator, Mother Earth, and each other. I was humbled by the kiva ceremony and inspired to strive for deeper purpose in my own life.

CHAPTER 17

A MYSTICAL EXPERIENCE IN THE DARK OF NIGHT

One of my female coworkers leaned her head in my office door and said, "A lady answered the phone, but she acted like there wasn't any meeting until I told her we were therapists on the Hopi land who are interested in the Red Road to Recovery."

That spiked my curiosity. "That's so interesting! So, I guess you got a meeting location?"

"Yes," she replied. "We're invited to the meeting tomorrow night."

The fellow therapist and I had been speculating about attending a meeting of Navajo elders in Tuba City ever since she saw an announcement in the newspaper. Our concern was that anyone who was not Navajo might not be welcomed to a Navajo elders' business and planning meeting. We had discussed this possible obstacle and hoped that we would be invited to attend because we wanted to learn more in order to help our clients. We both sincerely wanted to learn more about the Navajo strategies for helping young people live a spiritual and directed life, what they called the Red Road.

Tuba City was about an hour's drive northwest on Hwy. 264 from Second Mesa. If we left directly from work, we would arrive at the appointed time for the meeting. The meeting was to be held in a trailer beside a school building. We got out of the car and went up a few steps into the trailer. A Navajo man was sitting behind a folding table and looked up when we approached. We introduced ourselves and explained that we would like to attend that night's meeting. "There's no meeting here," he responded. We went through the same argument that my coworker had used with the lady on the phone, who had also initially denied the existence of a meeting. Finally, he acknowledged that a business meeting would begin in about twenty minutes and it would be okay for us to be present. I am telling you this to underscore how cautious the Navajo and Hopi people are when it comes to non-Natives attending any meeting or ceremony because of disrespect shown by so many in the past. This man was just preventing another possible insulting disregard for the sacredness of their beliefs and their culture.

After he had accepted our reason for interest in the meeting, the man who greeted us began to tell us about the posters on the walls of the room that was being used during the day for a school room. He told us that they were teaching the Navajo children their native language again. When the missionaries used coercion to take children to boarding schools, they would not allow them to speak their language. This reminded me of what the man who came to see me in my office had told me about his personal experience with boarding school. The greeter went on to say that the missionaries cut their hair, dressed them in uniforms, and told them that their cultural and religious beliefs, their language, their hair, and their dress were not what God intended and it was their mission to teach them the right way to live.

On the walls of the schoolroom was the Navajo language, a visual accompaniment to daily classes to teach Navajo children their native language and culture. We listened respectfully, and afterward we acknowledged how horrifying that treatment must have been for the Navajo people. To be stripped of everything you knew to be true and suddenly be taken away and basically be told that your former life was wicked and your parents were evil. As our greeter wound up his discussion of the intent of this additional schoolroom, Navajo male elders began to walk into the room.

The man behind the table told the elders that we could attend the meeting. A couple of men had black cowboy hats on and they acknowledged by nodding their heads. We followed them in and quietly took our seats. Nothing more was said until the meeting began. The leader of the meeting had a planned agenda with many topics to cover. Out of respect for the privacy of the Navajo people in the room, I will keep the content of the meeting confidential. We were privileged to be able to attend. Being able to listen to what was discussed increased my admiration for the Navajo people, who were working to maintain their culture for their children and for generations to come.

I will tell you that the group leader invited us to introduce ourselves and share our purpose for attending the meeting. We told the men that we were psychotherapists on the Hopi land working with Hopi and Navajo children and adults. Our intention was to add to our understanding of the culture and beliefs and future planning of the Native people, so that we could be more effective as we worked with our clients. Everyone listened politely and then the group leader went on to the next item on his agenda. This was another experience that added to my respect for Native people. After working all day, these men took the time to meet and plan for the future of their communities.

After the meeting ended, my friend and I went to a nearby diner for a light dinner. We shared our perspectives on what was helpful and what was especially interesting about the meeting and agreed that we were fortunate to be invited to attend. Hopefully, this was a small step in establishing trust. After finishing our meals, we drove an hour back to the Hopi land. The road out of Tuba City dropped south for a short distance and then turned east. We were on the Navajo land for the first thirty minutes of the hour drive. It was dark now and it seemed even darker because there were many miles between hogans, or trailers, on the Navajo land. We drove for miles in the dark without seeing any lights, except the headlights of the car. We didn't pass any cars and it was eerily quiet on the empty, flat, desolate road.

I was looking out the passenger-side window when I sensed an entity moving parallel to our car and at the same speed. I would guess it was about a mile away. I gave voice to my experience and broke the stillness by saying, "I don't want to scare you, but there is an entity of some sort out there. It is traveling at the same speed we are. I don't really see it, but I sense it."

"What do you mean? Where?" my travel companion asked.

"Out there about a mile or so away, moving parallel to us. I think I see a dark shape, but it doesn't really have a form. It's more like I sense it."

The driver took her eyes from the road long enough to stare out the passenger-side window, trying to see or feel or sense whatever it was that I knew was there. "I don't see anything," she said. She didn't argue that it wasn't there. She just didn't have the same experience that I was having. Perhaps if she had not been driving and was sitting on the passenger side, like I was, she would have also sensed the entity. At any rate, I felt compelled to say more about what I was experiencing.

"I don't feel scared. It's not evil and it's not going to harm us," I added. "I think that it is a force that is following us off the land, maybe to make sure we leave the land or maybe to be sure we are safe." My thoughts were that the spirit knew that we had been at a meeting with Navajo elders and that we had good intentions for wanting to attend. When we left the Navajo land boundary after traveling about thirty miles and entered the Hopi land, my feeling that we were being accompanied by a spirit dissipated. We still had about thirty more miles to go on the Hopi land before we got to the parking lot where my car was parked. No more words were spoken as we traveled from west to east on State Road 264 across the remote western part of the Hopi land.

That weekend, I decided to drive east on I-40 from my apartment in Flagstaff to a local trail for a walk. As I hiked, I mulled over the experiences of the mystical night on the Navajo land. I tend to think and rethink conversations, events, books I've read, and movies I've seen over and over in my mind. I have mulled over and analyzed the day's experiences since I was a child. I might be trying to figure out what was meant by a comment or I might be enjoying a particularly meaningful piece of dialogue as I play it in my mind again. Today, my mind and spirit were focused on the entity that I perceived on the Navajo land.

I was not shocked or alarmed that I had sensed an entity. I was just curious about what it was and what it meant. First of all, this was not my first time to feel energy. I thought back to walks in Ellijay and how I had a strong sense of energy at the lot in Walnut Mountain where only a chimney remained of someone's former home. My perception was that I felt the presence of the spirits of those who had occupied that space when it was their home. Another time, during a visit with Cousin Don, I stopped abruptly on a trail leading to Lake Meade when I felt intense energy. When I walked forward, it was gone. When I backed up to that same spot, I felt that same energy force again. Don had no idea what I was talking about when I explained my experience of sensing energy to him. Another incident happened when my friend JR and I were riding our motorcycles in Augusta, Georgia. I was following as he led us to a sort of cul-de-sac close to a park. He stopped and I stopped, too, but then quickly I told him that there was danger nearby, and we better move on.

My intense awareness of energy was validated by the teachings of Juan Matus, which were explained by Carlos Castaneda in his books. One of the experiential exercises that the seventy-year-old Yaqui seer Juan Matus taught was all about sensing energy. Juan led Carlos out into the wilderness to teach him how to be attuned to his environment. When he reached a resting place after walking for hours, Juan instructed Carlos to decide which rock to sit on based on sensing which energy attracted him. He was to walk around the small area until he knew where to sit based on his perception of the energy there. Juan's goal with this exercise was to teach Carlos to be aware of his surroundings and, more specifically, to sense the energy fields in different spaces.

Energy forces specific to Navajo spiritual beliefs are included in the cultural details that Tony Hillerman included in his mystery novels. Tony Hillerman's stories take place on the Navajo land. The main characters, who are members of the Navajo Tribal Police, travel across the Navajo land, seeking clues to solving crimes. As they travel, Hillerman skillfully and intentionally weaves in his love of the Southwest terrain and his love of the Navajo people. He includes Hopi and Zuni cultural and spiritual beliefs occasionally, too. His awareness and appreciation of the Navajo, Hopi, and Zuni people's ability to survive in harsh geographical conditions is apparent. What stands out starkly is his intent to convey his understanding of their spiritual beliefs and tribal traditions, to pass on his knowledge of their almost palpable sense of good and evil.

Beginning with his first book, *The Blessing Way*, in 1970, until his death in 2008, Hillerman fascinated his readers, including me, with descriptions of many spirits, from skinwalkers to shapeshifters. The spirits are deeply engrained in the beliefs of a people in tune with nature, who are also keen observers of human nature and of the spirit world. Joe Leaphorn, the older and more experienced police officer, understands the spiritual beliefs of the Navajo and incorporates his knowledge in solving crimes. When Hillerman introduced a younger police officer, Jim Chee, into the stories, he characterizes Chee as an intuitive vessel of spiritual beliefs. He has an uncanny gift for finding clues and solving murders because he understands the Navajo people and he lives their spiritual practices. I enjoyed Hillerman's books, not only because he could weave an interesting murder mystery, but because he encased the story in complex spiritual beliefs.

In addition to the influence of Hillerman's books, I had also been reading two books about the Hopi people since I first arrived in Flagstaff. One was a 1963 book by Frank Waters, titled *Book of the Hopi*, which I found in the gift shop in Flagstaff, and the other was *The Fourth World of the Hopis* (1987), written by Harold Courlander. The *Book of the Hopi* explains the creation story of the Hopi, the migration journey, and the settling of the Hopi into a land that they believe the Creator intended as their destination. In *The Fourth World of the Hopis*, Courlander dives deep into the interweaving of the migration journey with the importance of keeping a sense of continuity and a sense of identity. As I read both books, I was fascinated with the details of the history and the culture of the Hopi people, including belief in the supernatural.

I think that I perceived an energy force on the Navajo land for several reasons. I am naturally intuitive and I am open-minded about all kinds of ideas and experiences. I had read many books that alluded to spirits, both good and evil, being present in the environment. I had personally experienced the sacred energy of the Hopi land on my walks. I had worked closely with the Hopi and Navajo people and had observed that they lived their spirituality in their daily lives. I had witnessed the intense energy that was created in a sacred kiva ceremony. I had listened carefully when Hopi people told me about Kokopelli and kachinas and other spiritual archetypes, including Spider Woman and The Twins from the Hopi creation story. The spirits were tasked with generating energy forms, including sound and wind.

I knew that an energy force accompanied us off the Navajo land that night. That knowing told me as much about myself as it told me about the Navajo spirit world. I didn't feel alone in the world because I felt connected to the big web of existence. When I had a spiritual experience, especially when those around me didn't have the same experience, I thought about what that might mean. Like the Hopi and Navajo people, I believed that energy took many forms and had many purposes. I believed that I was an energy force and I was surrounded by energy forces. My beliefs and experiences were very much like those of the Hopi and Navajo people. In them, I saw myself.

CHAPTER 18

THE SAN FRANCISCO PEAKS AND THE FULL MOON

One morning in December of 1998, as the Hopi van made its way from Flagstaff to the Hopi land, I was astonished at the spectacular scene that met my northward gaze out the window. The San Francisco Peaks that provided a powerful backdrop to the town of Flagstaff were covered with snow and a gorgeous full moon was just to the right of the mountains, at the same elevation.

Many people on the van were making comments about the unusual occurrence. I was awestruck by the view for its jaw-dropping beauty, but also because it seemed to be a sign. *Look at this*, the Creator whispered to me. *Notice how balanced the full moon is with the mountains. These mountains are sacred to the Hopi and Navajo people and the cycles of the moon affect the earth and are guides for planting and the timing of rituals. The mountains and the moon are sending you a message about the importance of balance.* The Creator, the Artist, had created a scene that spoke to my soul. The deep meaning of the lessons that I was learning from the keenly observant Hopi people startled me and filled me with gratitude. Here was a caution sign about balance.

I realized that what seemed like a surprise was one of many unexpected experiences. The experiences working at the Hopi Guidance Center in Second Mesa, Arizona, had taught me to respect the wisdom and compassion of the Hopi people. I had entered what seemed like another world where the Hopis lived close to the earth, taking care of the environment and being cared for by the environment as a result of careful planning and hard work. Their intent to maintain balance and harmony through sacred rituals and ceremonies was meaningful to me. They knew their purpose and they knew that in this place, this sacred Hopi land, they were meant to fulfill their destiny. I was here to learn from them.

A belief in the Creator of all life and a belief that all of nature must live together in balance, the water, the trees, the rocks, the plants, and the people, fueled their passion for a give-and-take relationship and connection with the Earth Mother. Their spiritual lives and their practical daily lives were one and the same. Growing the corn was a mission that sustained their people and reflected their clever approach to working with the land. They honored the Creator and all creation with their grit and determination. They honored their ancestors who migrated in the four directions to follow their destiny with unquestioning faith in their sacred destiny. Staying true to their past, working hard in the present, and planning for the future, they maintained their villages through the efforts and talents of all of the clans. As the wise Hopi woman said, "I was born for the Bear clan."

From observing the Hopi with solemn regard, I had learned more about who I was. I had discovered my authentic self by reflecting on my past, honoring my ancestors, and listening to the Creator, whose presence was so strong on this powerful land. I was given certain talents for a reason. My responsibility, like the Hopi, was to appreciate my heritage, live up to my potential, and strive to maintain balance by prioritizing my spiritual beliefs, living in harmony with the earth, with myself, and with others. I had learned to honor my Daddy's words, "Someday you will be a writer." The idea for a book came to life in Ellijay and I was actually writing the book in Flagstaff. I was a gardener of the Earth just as my mother and my Auntie Grace had been gardeners. I loved to dig in the dirt, plant seeds, and watch them grow, just as the Creator intended.

Like the Hopi, I was not impressed with the material world or status. On the Hopi land, everyone lived humbly. There were no fancy hotels or restaurants. The elders and shamans lived like everyone else. In the kivas, the leaders were literally at the same level as the others. They were not raised above, looking down at anyone. In fact, the Hopis literally walked down ladders into the earth for their rituals and ceremonies, where they danced and chanted to keep the earth balanced on its axis and to summon the spirits to reciprocate their efforts with rain, crops, and harmony.

Because I had taken risks moving to Ellijay without knowing anyone or having a job and then traveled to Arizona without being sure of a job, I had experiences that expanded my thinking and I met wonderful people who inspired me. I got answers to questions like "Who am I?" and "What is my purpose?" I met other unconventional people, other nonconformists, who were truly kindred spirits. Painful situations like the divorce from Mark and extreme frustration at work pushed me to make huge changes, to move toward the unknown, searching for answers. I moved from one place to another, as the Hopi people had done, migrating in many directions before finding their current location in northeastern Arizona. It seemed that I had to travel long distances to find myself and my destiny.

My journey led me to the freedom of riding my motorcycle everywhere and living in a log cabin in the woods. I figured out how to connect with kindred spirits by starting a book discussion group. I created a women's personal and spiritual growth group to study and learn and brainstorm ideas with other women in search of knowledge and wisdom. I started my own therapy business where I felt that I made a difference in people's lives. I communed with nature during many long walks in my community in the North Georgia Mountains and long walks on the Hopi land. By exploring, I found my authentic self, the inquisitive, open-minded woman on a quest for meaning.

I found work that matched my values, both in my own private practice and as a mental health counselor with the Hopis. In both environments, I experienced a sense of purpose and knew that I was utilizing my skills to help others. I took the time for solitude to reflect on the influence of my ancestors and to commit myself to carrying on a legacy of risk-takers and hard workers. From my paternal great-grandmother bringing her children on a ship from Sweden to America, to my grandfather taking the chance to leave Scotland and take root in America, to crazy Cousin Don, who drove throughout the United States camping with his dog, visiting family, and working as an electrician and cameraman, my ancestors were adventurous risk-takers.

My distress about the divorce with Mark disappeared when I looked at the big picture of my life. Mark and I met for a reason. He represented freedom with his backstory of leaving his birthplace, Finland, in his twenties and coming to the United States, land of opportunities. He encouraged me to ride my own motorcycle and he asked, "When are you going to write a book?" In the bigger scheme of life, he was a messenger who had remained a close friend. That's how to move on in relationships, I learned. Look at the bigger picture, absorb what I learned from that person that helped me to evolve, then move forward to the next step.

From having my own business in Ellijay and working with the Hopis at Behavioral Health Services, I learned that I could thrive when I respected the work ethic and values of my colleagues and when I was doing meaningful work. I didn't have to have my own business, but I did have to know that the values of the work environment correlated with my values.

Most of all, I learned to focus on my spiritual life, as Carlos Castenada taught me in his books. He called the mundane, everyday life the "tonal" and the spiritual mystery of life the "nagual," and he stressed the importance of focusing most of my attention on the nagual. Life was a great mystery, as he said, a wonderfully fascinating mystery. Looking at the beautiful San Francisco Peaks and the almost surreal full moon, I was reminded of the spiritual importance of the mountains to the Hopi and the Navajo and how the Hopi are guided by the phases of the moon as they plant and harvest. The Hopis knew that powerful forces were at work and that working in balance with those forces would create harmony. As Carlos Castaneda learned from the Yaqui and I learned from the Hopi people, reality encompasses much more than most of us realize.

I started this journey on a quest to answer mundane questions and I quickly expanded my attention to a much bigger reality. There was so much to explore, places, people, ideas. Right now, in this moment with the startling gorgeous mountain and the full moon, I knew that I was destined to come here and that I still had much to learn. I had been working with the Hopi people for about three months. Even though I had begun to clarify who I was and what I was born to accomplish, I knew that balance and harmony were not even on my radar.

Learning about the importance of balance and harmony from the Hopis and witnessing the application of those values in their lives had not yet translated into action on my part. That would become clear in the weeks ahead.

CHAPTER 19

OUT OF BALANCE

I was not in balance when I moved to Ellijay and I wasn't in balance when I arrived in Arizona. Figuring out how to be true to myself and devote enough time to my family left me mystified. When I moved to Ellijay, I talked with my children about the option of moving there, but I made the decision impulsively without considering their feelings. When I decided to go to Arizona, I just informed them that I was going and when I would leave. Balancing time for family, time for work, and time for myself was a struggle for me. When I took time for myself, I was not spending enough time with my family. My attraction to men who did not have my best interests in mind also got me off track, as I mentioned in chapter 9, Daddy's Letters.

I flew home to Georgia for the Christmas holiday, intending to spend time with my family. I only spent Christmas afternoon exchanging gifts with my children and granddaughter. I had spent a lot of time preparing for the visit, buying and wrapping Christmas presents that I purchased at one of the Hopi gift shops, but I only spent a few hours with my family. I don't know what I was thinking. *Oh, yes, I know what happened*, I thought. *I spread my time and energy in too many directions. My priorities are out of balance.*

I also developed a cold with a persistent cough while I was in Georgia. I guess my body felt out of balance too. That hacking cough continued for a month after my return to work with the

Hopis, causing fatigue and loss of sleep. The Behavioral Health Department director, Georgia Yukiwma, had a similar cough, and we commiserated about the difficulty of concentrating on our work when we didn't feel well. I tried many remedies and nothing helped in alleviating the cough. Then, menopause showed up. The imbalance of periods that were heavy one day and almost nonexistent the next was exasperating. I did find a remedy, dong quai root. Many cups of hot tea helped to even out my hormones. My body and my mind were out of balance.

My financial situation was also precarious. I had traded car payments on one car for lease payments on another. Just like many single women, I had bills like car insurance, gasoline, car maintenance, apartment rent, utilities, and phone bills, and I continued to send my ex-husband money to help with the care of our thirteen-year-old son, Trey. Then there was the money for the typing and formatting of my *Tools for Living* book. I chose not to buy any furniture except the futon, which served as a sofa and bed. The kitchen counter with barstools doubled for eating and for studying. What I started realizing was that I didn't have any cushion if something unexpected happened.

I thought about the recent phone call from Heather telling me that she was going to go back to school to get an advanced degree in information technology. With hours of classes and studying, she needed my help with childcare. Now it was time to get specific about a plan to drive back to Georgia at the end of March. Some of my stuff was still stored in the outdoor building at Mark's place north of Phoenix, so I would get a trailer and a hitch in Phoenix, load up my few belongings and my motorcycle, and drive the two or three days back home. Heather offered for me to stay with her until I found an apartment and got a job.

The morning of Monday, March 1, 1999, I met with my supervisor and told her that I was going to go back to Georgia and gave a month's work notice. I explained that my daughter needed help with the care of my granddaughter, since she was going to take classes to get another degree. I told her how much I had enjoyed working with her and with the other staff members and how much I appreciated the opportunity that I was given. The Saturday before that, during my book-writing coffee klatch at Timberline Village Apartments, I had talked with Justine about my decision to head back to Georgia the end of March. She had the paperwork stating that I was not continuing the lease on my apartment after the month of March ready to sign on Monday evening.

I knew that even though I loved working with the Hopis more than I could have imagined and had entertained ideas of extending my stay, I would go back home as originally planned. I really loved the Southwest, the landscape with its rugged black mountains and desert and mesas, the red rock of Sedona. I loved Flagstaff, its stunning beauty, the San Francisco Peaks, and the casual feel of the town and its people. I felt the vibrant energy in this part of the country that drew me in, that pulled at me to stay. I also loved the Hopi and Navajo people. They were warm and caring, intelligent and resourceful. Their sense of purpose and their persistence to live their legacy inspired me. I could have stayed there. I could have stayed there a very long time. But the whispered words of the Creator cautioning me about attaining balance as I had gazed at the San Francisco Peaks and the full moon weighed on me. The Creator spoke to me and sent me a sign. Get your life in balance. My body had been ill with an exhausting cough and the symptoms of menopause foretold of transition. My mind was telling me that I had to make some changes to establish balance and achieve harmony with myself, with my family, and with the Creator's design for my life.

I spent my remaining time in Arizona finishing the writing of *Tools for Living* and getting it typed and formatted. I started working on my income tax, planning to get the necessary documents to a CPA shortly after I returned to Georgia. Before I left Arizona, I spent time with my friends in Flagstaff. In the evenings after work, I went to the apartment complex gym. On the weekend, I joined some Flagstaff friends as we hiked up the San Francisco

Peaks to where the snow started. One Saturday evening some friends from the apartment complex and I donned sombreros for a chain dance at a local restaurant. I returned to the Irish pub for Irish stew and the music of a couple who played guitar and sang.

While spending time with the members of the Hopi and the Navajo tribes, I soaked in the beauty of the land and listened as the three mesas spoke to me of spirits and the Creator's purpose. I thought of the Native people with their allegiance to family and their legacy of following in the footsteps of their ancestors, doing what they were born to do, living the way they were born to live. I wanted to take it all in, to incorporate their values into my life. I wanted to be in balance and to live in harmony. Getting closer to that goal would come after my return to Georgia. In the meantime, I continued reading the *Book of the Hopi* and started reading novels by Tony Hillerman that focus on Navajo culture and also include Hopi land and culture. Before my return, I wanted to experience and learn as much as I could. I planned one more excursion.

Chapter 20

Window Rock

Window Rock, Arizona, was the location of the Navajo Tribal Police Headquarters, where Lieutenant Joe Leaphorn has his office in the Tony Hillerman novels. While reading *The Blessing Way*, Hillerman's first novel in the Joe Leaphorn/Jim Chee series, I had pictured the large opening eroded out of a sandstone cliff. I imagined Joe Leaphorn, who was born into the Slow Talking People clan and lived on the Navajo land, solving murder mysteries using his firsthand knowledge of the Navajo people, their culture, and the terrain. On a Saturday in March, 1999, I was in Window Rock to see the stomping grounds of Joe Leaphorn for myself.

The forty-seven-foot opening that looked like a window in the two-hundred-foot-tall cliff had been eroded by winds over many years. More spectacular up close and personal, the sight alone was worth the three-hour drive from Flagstaff east almost to the New Mexico border. What interested me most, though, was the Navajo cultural and spiritual beliefs that Leaphorn wove into his analysis of the complexities of who, what, where, and why. Just as the wind allowed light to come through the sandstone structure, I hoped that being in Joe Leaphorn's base of operations would bring me an increased understanding of the Navajo beliefs.

As I entered a building dedicated to Navajo culture, I was drawn to a Navajo woman sitting in front of a large loom, weaving a blanket of brown, black, and sand colors. I walked toward her, found a place to stand and watch, and was soon mesmerized as she added one row after another to the design. Her skill and the intricacy of the design captured my attention for a long time. I watched her work until she came to the final row, where I was surprised to see her weave a hole that did not match the rest of the design before completing the blanket. When she had finished her work and put her hands in her lap, I felt comfortable talking with her.

"Your blanket is so beautiful," I said. "I am curious why you left a place that was different from the rest. It looked like you did it on purpose."

She replied that she intentionally left a small hole to share the Navajo belief that nothing and no one is perfect. The Navajo people, she explained, used their skills to make objects that serve a purpose and bring beauty, as the Creator intended. Her humble perspective on life was inspiring to me. The blanket's purpose was not to draw attention to her and her skill, but to help others by bringing warmth and beauty and sharing Navajo beliefs in the design. I thanked the Navajo woman for her time and went to look at other Navajo creations. Jewelry crafted by a Navajo man was on display on a table across the room. I noticed a silver bracelet with many designs, including a black swastika. Because I had been reading *Book of the Hopi* by Frank Waters, I knew that the swastika dated back thousands of years before Hitler demonized the symbol.

I was curious what the swastika meant to the Navajo. I introduced myself and admired his bracelets and necklaces. "I wonder what the swastika symbolizes to the Navajo and why you included it on this bracelet." To the Navajo, he explained, the "Whirling Log" is a sacred image associated with healing rituals. It includes references to the rotation of life and to the four directions, but the significance is its representation of well-being and protection. "That is so interesting. Thank you."

As I walked out of the building and looked around, I soaked in the energy of this space. I was thankful to be in Window Rock, and thought of how an author's fictional stories brought me here to learn more about the Navajo people, their spiritual beliefs, and the land that Tony Hillerman described in such breathtaking detail in his books. I found a diner to have a quick lunch before driving back to Flagstaff. As I drove, I thought of my experiences in Window Rock and I planned to read again the pages in *Book of the Hopi* that taught what the swastika means to the Hopi people.

The next morning, I put the coffeemaker to work brewing while I assembled paper, pen, and some books on the kitchen counter. I was going to spend Sunday doing some more research, taking some notes, and mulling over my thoughts about my experiences in Window Rock. I decided to focus on the two experiences that stood out in my mind, the Navajo woman's words about the purpose of creating blankets and the Navajo man's explanation of the symbolism of the swastika in Navajo culture. Sitting on a barstool with a cup of black coffee on the counter and a pen in my hand, I reflected on the wise words about imperfection and selfless intentions.

> *Perfection is not important to the Navajo not because it is not achievable, but because it involves ego. The Navajo weaver was not displaying her blanket and her craftsmanship to say, "Look at me. Look at how smart and skilled I am. Look at this beautiful blanket that I made with my own hands." No, she taught me that the purpose for crafting a blanket was not to glorify or bring attention to herself. The purpose was to add warmth, beauty, and meaning to the lives of those around her.*

I thought about how humble she was and how dedicated she was to making a difference in other people's lives. She was carrying on a tradition of service that she learned from her ancestors. Like the Hopi woman who told us that she was born *for* her clan, this woman knew that her purpose was predestined, determined by her ancestors, who passed their values down through the generations. There was no individual ego involved. There were no egotistical thoughts about what others thought of her. She purposefully and intentionally carried out the work that would contribute to the survival and enjoyment of her community and others.

> *When I become clear about my purpose on this planet, then will I no longer get off track in my actions? Can I get so focused on what I am supposed to be contributing with my life that no person or activity can sway me off course? Will I choose only to associate with those who support me and contribute to my life's purpose? That was my goal. I wanted to emulate this woman and the Navajo way of thinking.*

I knew that I would continue to make mistakes on my quest to self-discovery. Just as the hole in the blanket symbolized imperfection, my goal could not be perfection. My goal was to make progress in my evolvement as a spiritual being navigating the planet in a human body. I would still get distracted and let go of the wheel, but my efforts to learn and to grow would move me forward. I was inspired by the Navajo people, who were exerting such effort to hang on to their culture, to teach their children the Navajo language and the customs of their ancestors. I was awestruck by their awareness of the sacredness of all life, from horses and sheep to the dog that Jeremiah blessed with corn pollen. They were carrying on the values of their ancestors and the mission that the Creator bestowed on them—to contribute to the greater good.

As I stepped off the kitchen barstool to get another cup of coffee, my thoughts shifted to the Navajo jewelry maker and his explanation of the swastika in the Navajo culture. When I sat back down, I opened *Book of the Hopi* to refresh myself on the Hopi significance of the swastika symbol. The Hopi migration story symbolized by the swastika has been passed down from one generation to another for at least nine hundred years. The Hopis arrived in Old Oraibi no later than 1100 AD after a long migration journey that took the twelve clans in four directions. According to the author, some clans turned right before retracing their steps and other clans turned left. Thus, one version of the swastika migration symbol turns clockwise and the other version turns counterclockwise. The center of the symbol, representing where the Hopi ultimately settled, is believed to be the spiritual and magnetic center where the clans were led by the Creator to fulfill their purpose.

My soul-searching journey had led me in many directions. I traveled north to Ellijay, Georgia, where the seeds to my first book were planted and where I started a book discussion group and a women's personal and spiritual growth group. Then I traveled west-northwest to Second Mesa, Arizona, where I worked for the Hopi Behavioral Health Department and learned about the Hopi closeness to Mother Earth and dedication to maintaining balance and harmony. From there, I drove west to Tuba City, where I attended a Navajo business meeting and learned of the Navajo efforts to teach their children the Navajo language and culture, so that the Navajo culture and beliefs continue for generations. Next, I traveled east to Window Rock, where I learned two lessons. First, a Navajo woman taught me about the acknowledgment of imperfection and the importance of a selfless life of service, spreading beauty and carrying on the Navajo beliefs. Then, a Navajo man enlightened me about the ancient meaning of the "whirling logs" swastika symbol in the Navajo culture.

The Hopi were guided by the Creator to travel in four directions before ending their migration journey in Old Oraibi, Arizona, and spreading from there to the present locations of their twelve villages. I don't know if my travels were divinely directed, like the Hopi, or if I decided to travel many places because of restlessness, curiosity, or intuition. But I do know that I made discoveries about myself because I took risks and made choices to travel to the North Georgia Mountains and to the Hopi and Navajo lands in Arizona. I met people, teachers really, who guided and inspired me. I was exposed to cultures whose beliefs coincided with what I believed. I felt at home with the Hopi and the Navajo people. I was a kindred spirit. I walked on sacred lands whose intense spiritual energy grabbed my soul. I found myself.

EPILOGUE

My journey of self-discovery lasted five years, from April 1994 to March 1999, and took me from Georgia to the Hopi and Navajo lands and back to Georgia. I traveled a total of 4,200 miles, not counting all the trips back and forth from Flagstaff, Arizona, where I stayed in an apartment at Timberline Village, to Second Mesa, Arizona, where I worked at Pa'angni, the Hopi Guidance Center. With every stop along the way, I clarified who I was and what gave my life meaning. My epiphanies validated that I was an unconventional, nonconformist, risk-taking woman whose curiosity and search for knowledge could not be quenched. I began to figure out what I was born to accomplish. My first purpose was to write books that inspire others to be authentic and hopeful, to be open-minded and eager to learn, and to evolve spiritually. My second contribution was to share what I had learned and to spark life-changing discussions through women's personal and spiritual growth groups. Third, I was passionate about living close to the land and planting vegetable and flower gardens. In this role, I felt that I was doing my part in maintaining the cycle of life by planting the seed that the Creator provides, nurturing the plants that emerge from the Earth, and reaping the harvest to feed my family and share with my community. I began to sense energy in people and energy of specific places. Being with the Hopis and the Navajo increased my desire to evolve spiritually and the energy of their sacred lands held me in awe.

I finished writing *Tools for Living: Taking Control of Your Life* after I returned to Georgia. I searched for someone to type the final copy and coordinate the numerous steps to completion and I found Marci Rheinschild. Marci was a creative woman who lived on a sheep farm with her husband and children. She was a Master Gardener who grew all kinds of colorful flowers to make dye for her yarn. She sheared her own sheep and spun and dyed the natural fiber. In addition, she ran a graphic company out of her home in northeast Georgia.

I made many trips to her farm on my motorcycle, packing pages of content and notes and ideas in the saddlebags. We worked together to select the paper weight and color for the pages, the thick brown paper for the front and back covers, and we decided to make the seventy-four-page self-help book spiral-bound. I ordered the ISBN numbers myself and received a long roll of stick-on barcodes with the ISBN number on top. I literally stuck the barcode and ISBN stickers on the back cover of each book manually. Marci coordinated with a company to print the pages, another to make the cover, and another to bind the book. This long process was completed in November 2000, when I became an author. This was before I knew about print-on-demand, so the book was available only in paperback, not online. I borrowed money, ordered one thousand copies, and crossed my fingers that I could sell them. Bookstores were very accommodating by allowing me to do book signings, and several bookstores and gift shops kept an inventory of the books and called me when they wanted more.

Instead of continuing to write two more books in a trilogy of *Tools for Living* books, which I had originally planned, my next self-help book was *Think Your Way to Happiness: Strategies for an Enjoyable, Meaningful Life* (2020), which expanded on many of the tools in *Tools for Living*. As I was writing this memoir, I had the idea to revise and update *Tools for Living*. Frankly, I hoped that some of you who read this memoir might be curious about the content of my first book. In 2023, *Tools for Living* was brought back to life with revisions and updates and a shiny new cover. The book has come full circle, from my first book written in longhand and then typed, to a digitally available book today.

The writing of this memoir, *Digging Deeper*, has taken over two years, starting as a chronological account of the various experiences that demonstrate what a nontraditional maverick I was, and, over time, evolving to a much deeper, reflective, insightful quest for meaning. I was digging deeper, spending more time contemplating and pondering than I did pounding the keys on my computer. This book has been a process of self-realization, of soul-searching, of digging deeper and deeper as I reread letters, looked at old photos, studied journals, reviewed women's group agendas, and spent hours thinking and thinking. I was surprised by the discoveries I made about myself, my purpose, and how my life has hopefully made a difference.

In addition to continuing to write books, I also continued to create and facilitate women's personal and spiritual growth groups. I picked up where I left off with the Ellijay group when I returned to Georgia. I started by calling the women who were in the group that met at my Ellijay office before I left for Arizona. Since I no longer had an office, one of the women secured a room at the Unitarian Universalist Church in Ellijay, which was kindly donated free of charge. I got busy putting together new themes, and discussion points, and suggested readings. My computer skills had improved since the Hopi Tribe had sent me to Northern Arizona University for a day of computer training, so my agendas looked more professional. But, more importantly, I had grown and evolved in my thinking. An impetus for leaving Ellijay and working with the Hopi and Navajo was my desire to learn more so that I could share more new ideas.

I not only felt confident that I had more to contribute to women's groups after my travels, but I had an increased passion about the importance of coming together in small groups to support and learn from each other. I vividly remembered feeling an urgency to get groups going again after walking out of a home on the Hopi land where I had met with a female Hopi teenager and her family. I was thinking how helpful it would have been for that young woman to connect with other teenagers in a small group where she would feel comfortable sharing her thoughts. In Dawsonville, Georgia, I had the opportunity to start a second women's group. In the building where I rented office space for my therapy business, I had access to a conference room. In that space, a group of eager and curious women gathered to listen to my ideas and discuss them. The logo that they created for their group was Meadowlarks: A Cheerful Journey Inward.

In 2015, I put together a women's group in Gainesville, Georgia, where Larry and I had moved in 2012 and where we live now. That group of bright and interesting women met for a year until my space became too small. We transitioned to meeting at one of the women's homes for a while, until she decided to downsize and move into a smaller home. I didn't pursue finding another space because gardening had begun to consume much more of my time and energy.

My time and energy flowed into my ever-expanding vegetable and flower garden behind our small farmhouse in Gainesville, Georgia. I began with a small garden spot in 2013, and now, ten years later, the garden has expanded, thanks to Larry's efforts to fence and till a bigger area. Our house is 900 square feet and the area of our garden is 1,800 square feet. This contributes to the balance and harmony in my life.

My sweetheart, Larry, and my black cat, Kiki, and I enjoy being in the energy of all the plants that are growing with the help of the sun and the rain and the fertile, compost-fed soil. Gardening also takes me back in time to the happy hours spent tending the vegetable garden with Mother at my childhood home in Arlington, Texas. She taught me to turn the soil and harvest the crops and appreciate fresh vegetables on the table. We didn't have a tiller then. We worked the soil with a garden fork. I still work the periphery of the garden, along the fence line, with a garden fork just because I enjoy it. Auntie Grace, Mother's older sister, who lived in New Haven, Connecticut, taught me about the beauty and fragrant scents of flower gardens, which she described as "pungent." I spent many hours in her garden with a white arching rose arbor covered with pink roses. She planted blue spruce trees that gave privacy to the backyard and a border for her gorgeous flower beds. She created her gardens with ideas and hard work.

My mother and my aunt, living in different parts of the country, yet both creating gardens. And here I am in Gainesville, Georgia, creating an ever-expanding garden. I am reminded of the Hopi matrilinear progression of values and skills from mother to daughter, on and on for generations. I was fortunate that my ancestors taught me how to garden and instilled the value of gardening. As I sit in the garden on my Adirondack bench shaded by banana trees, I think of how I was inspired to grow bigger gardens by the zealous and industrious Hopis. When I watched the piles of blue corn grow higher and higher on Hopi porches, I was inspired to grow more vegetables for the sustenance of my family and the enjoyment of neighbors and friends.

This year I am growing Hopi blue corn in honor of my Hopi friends. I was fortunate that my daughter's friend in New Mexico gave me the blue corn seed when we visited Laurie Grace last November. I planted the corn in circles of five seeds each, four circles to a row, three rows. When all the corn seeds didn't germinate from the first planting, I replanted in the empty spaces and soon more sprouts pushed their way through the soil. Now, in July, the cornstalks are proudly reaching higher every day, showing off their tassels. On most of the stalks, corn silks have appeared and ears of corn are forming. I am amazed at the strength of these corn plants. They stood strong through a storm with high winds and heavy rains. That same storm knocked my sunflowers flat on the ground. The roots of the cornstalks are almost as big around as a pencil and have clawed deeply into the earth. Each seed has produced four to five stalks. This morning I pulled the first ear of corn from one of the plants. I spread the husks away to reveal beautiful blue corn on a cob almost a foot long.

So, twenty-four years after my journey, I still share my thoughts with books, hoping to inspire. I look back fondly to the women who connected and exchanged ideas in the groups. I grow my summer and fall gardens, enjoying digging deeper each year. Digging deeper for new ways to write, new ways to share ideas, new ways to grow vegetables and flowers. I am digging deeper for meaning and continuing to learn about myself and about life.

Acknowledgments

Thank you to family and friends who encouraged and supported me.

My sweetheart, Larry, kept a roof over my head and gave me love and affection while I spent hours in my office with doors closed. He never complained and often filled in by going to the grocery store and grilling dinner. You always have my back. I love you so much.

My daughters, Heather and Laurie Grace, spent countless hours reading the manuscript and making very detailed suggestions for changes. You asked questions that helped me think about clarity and flow. You shared your thoughts on the phone and in person. You brought out the heart and soul of this book.

My friends in my writing group, the Northeast Georgia Writers, were so supportive, asking sincere questions about my progress, discussing difficulties in the writing process, and adding, "I can't wait to read the book!" That means so much.

The BookLogix team worked their magic in transforming words on a page into this book. Many people devoted their time and talent in a collaborative effort, and someone was always available by phone or email.

Stan Hester, Stan Hester Photography in Lilburn, Georgia, did a great job on the author photo and is also a great guy.

Thank you to everyone who asked, "How's the book coming?" Those words kept me going and often got me back on track when I was feeling overwhelmed.

Books That Inspired Me on My Journey

These are some of the books I read on my journey of self-discovery. I have listed the books in the order that I read them.

The Celestine Prophecy, James Redfield
The Teachings of Don Juan: A Yaqui Way of Knowledge, Carlos Castaneda
Jonathon Livingston Seagull, Richard Bach
Illusions, Richard Bach
The 7 Habits of Highly Effective People, Stephen Covey
Circle of Stones, Judith Duerk
Sacred Path Cards, Jamie Sams
Stations of Solitude, Alice Koller
Women Who Run with the Wolves, Clarissa Estes
A Return to Love, Marianne Williamson
The Power of the Mind to Heal, Joan Borysenko
First You Have to Row a Little Boat, Richard Bode
The Dragon Doesn't Live Here Anymore, Alan Cohen
The Seven Spiritual Laws of Success, Deepak Chopra
Care of the Soul, Thomas Moore
Fire in the Soul, Joan Borysenko
Half Asleep in Frog Pajamas, Tom Robbins
Women's Bodies, Women's Wisdom, Christine Northrupp
Conversations with God, Neale Donald Walsch
Anatomy of the Spirit, Carolyn Myss
Second Sight, Judith Orloff
The Re-Enchantment of Everyday Life, Thomas Moore
Everyday Tao: Living with Balance and Harmony, Ding Ming-Dao

Transforming Pain into Power, Doris Helge
Succulent Wild Women, SARK
The Four Agreements, Miguel Ruiz
Affirmations, Stuart Wilde
Earth Dance Drum: A Celebration of Life, Blackwolf and Gina Jones
Book of the Hopi, Frank Waters
The Fourth World of the Hopi, Harold Courlander

ABOUT THE AUTHOR

Laurie Hyatt, PhD, is the author of four books, *Silent Decision: Awareness Out of Tragedy*, *Think Your Way to Happiness: Strategies for an Enjoyable, Meaningful Life*, *Tools for Living: Taking Control of Your Life*, and *Digging Deeper: Finding Myself on Hopi and Navajo Land*. She holds a doctoral degree in educational psychology from the University of Georgia, which she attained when she was sixty years old. As an adjunct faculty member, she taught psychology classes at many colleges and universities, including the University of North Georgia, Scottsdale Community College, and Chandler-Gilbert Community College in Arizona, and she served as assistant professor of psychology at Barton College in Wilson, North Carolina.

As a licensed professional counselor, she had therapy offices in Ellijay, Dawsonville, and Gainesville, Georgia, where she also created and facilitated women's personal and spiritual growth groups.

Laurie is an avid vegetable and flower gardener. She lives with her sweetheart, Larry, and their black cat, Kiki, in Gainesville, Georgia.

www.ingramcontent.com/pod-product-compliance
Lightning Source LLC
Chambersburg PA
CBHW060603080526
44585CB00013B/670